Lord Be Merciful

Selected Writings of
A.W. Tozer

Lord Be Merciful

Selected Writings of A.W. Tozer

The Pursuit of God

Keys to the Deeper Life

How to be Filled With the Holy Spirit

&

The Christian Book of Mystical Verse

by

A. W. Tozer

Copyright © 2021 Mockingbird Press

All rights reserved. The original works are in the public domain to the best of publisher's knowledge. The publisher makes no claim to the original writings. However, the compilation, construction, cover design, trademarks, derivations, foreword, descriptions, added work, etc., of this edition are copyrighted and may not be reproduced, distributed, or transmitted in any form or by any means, including photocopying, recording, or other electronic or mechanical methods, without the prior written permission of the publisher, except in the case of brief quotations embodied in critical reviews and certain other non-commercial uses permitted by copyright law, or where content is specifically noted as being reproduced under a Creative Commons license.

Cover, "Teich am Abend," by Christian Rohlfs, 1896
Cover Design by Matthew Johnson, Copyright © 2021 Mockingbird Press
Foreword by Rachael Underhill, Copyright © 2021 Mockingbird Press

Publisher's Cataloging-In-Publication Data

Tozer, A.W., author; with Underhill, Rachael, foreword by
Lord Be Merciful : Selected Writings of A.W. Tozer: The Pursuit of God, Keys to the Deeper Life, How to be Filled with the Holy Spirit, and The Christian Book of Mystical Verse / A.W. Tozer; with Rachael Underhill.

Paperback	ISBN-13: 978-1-953450-83-8
Hardback	ISBN-13: 978-1-953450-84-5
Ebook	ISBN-13: 978-1-953450-85-2

1. Religion—Christian Living—General. 2. Philosophy & Religion—Religion & Beliefs—Christianity—Christian Life & Practice, I. Author A.W. Tozer. II. Rachael Underhill. III. Lord Be Merciful. IV. Title : Selected Writings of A.W. Tozer: The Pursuit of God, Keys to the Deeper Life, How to be Filled with the Holy Spirit, and The Christian Book of Mystical Verse

REL012000 / QRMP

Type Set in Century Schoolbook / **Franklin Gothic Demi**

Mockingbird Press, Augusta, GA
info@mockingbirdpress.com

Contents

Foreword xi

The Pursuit of God

Introduction 3
Preface 5
Following Hard After God 7
The Blessedness of Possessing Nothing 13
Removing the Veil 19
Apprehending God 27
The Universal Presence 33
The Speaking Voice 39
The Gaze of the Soul 45
Restoring the Creator-creature Relation 52
Meekness and Rest 58
The Sacrament of Living 63

Keys to the Deeper Life

No Revival Without Reformation 71
The Deeper Life: What is it? 76
Gifts Of The Spirit: Are They For Us Today? 81
How To Be Filled With The Spirit 86

How to be Filled with the Holy Spirit

Preface 93
Who is the Holy Spirit? 94
The Promise of the Father 100
How to be Filled, with the Holy Spirit 106
How to Cultivate the Spirit's Companionship 111

The Christian Book Of Mystical Verse

Adoration Of The Godhead 122
    Eternal Power!... 122
    Lord Of All Being... 123
    Adoration 123
    The Unity Of God 124
    The Holy Trinity 125
    Majesty Divine!... 127
    The Vision Of The Godhead 129
    The Thought Of God.. 131
    The Greatness Of God... 133
    The Eternity Of God.. 135
    The Fear Of God 137
    The Eternal Father 139
    The Eternal Generation Of The Son 141
    The Holy Spirit 143
    Pentecost... 145

Devotional Meditations On The Cross Of Christ 147
    If Sweet The Moments, Rich In Blessing................................. 147
    Ride On! Ride On In Majesty!.. 148
    Would Jesus Have The Sinner Die? 148
    He Dies! The Friend Of Sinners Dies!...................................... 150
    Before The Cross 151
    O Sacred Head, Now Wounded.. 151
    Not All The Blood Of Beasts 152

Penitential Reflections On Our Sins.. 154
    My Sins, My Saviour!.. 154
    Have Mercy, God Most High 155
    O Lord, I Am Ashamed To Seek Thy Face............................... 156
    Scourge, But Receive Me.. 157

Rejoicing In Forgiveness And Justification............................... 158
    Song Of Assurance.. 158

    A Good Confession 159
    A Soul In Its Earliest Love 160

Yearning For Purity Of Heart 162
    I Thirst, Thou Wounded Lamb Of God 162
    Prayer For Purity 163
    Jesus, Thine All-Victorious Love 164
    Self-Love 165

Aspirations After God 167
    As Pants The Hart 167
    The Way Of Perfection 168
    Thou Shepherd Of Israel, And Mine 169
    The Fervor Of Holy Desire 170
    Desire Of God 171
    Satisfied 173

Delighting In God's Presence 175
    God Is Present Everywhere 175
    The Royal Priesthood 176
    God Reveals His Presence 176
    Within The Holy Place 177
    Lo, God Is Here! 178
    Allured Into The Desert 178

The Raptures Of Divine Love 180
    O Love Divine! 180
    I Love My God 181
    The Acquiescence Of Pure Love 181
    Jesus, Thy Boundless Love To Me 182
    O Love Divine! 183
    The Hidden Love Of God 184
    Love's Immensity 185

The Rest Of Faith 186
    All Must Be Well 186
    Confidence 187

Sometimes A Light Surprises 188
　　　The Blessed Journey 188
　　　Jesus, I Am Resting, Resting 189
　　　Resignation 190
　　　In Heavenly Love Abiding 191
　　　The Remembrance Of Mercy 192
The Spiritual Warfare 193
　　　Distractions In Prayer 193
　　　The Benefits Of Suffering 195
　　　Sorrow And Love 196
Victory Through Praise 197
　　　Come, O My Soul 197
　　　Bless, O My Soul, The Living God 198
　　　I'll Praise My Maker 198
　　　I Sing Th' Almighty Power Of God 199
　　　Now Thank We All Our God 200
　　　Te Deum Laudamus 201
The Prayer Of Quiet 203
　　　The Spirit Of Prayer 203
　　　My God! Silent To Thee! 203
　　　God's Eternal Now 204
　　　My Heart Is Resting, O My God 205
　　　Hidden In God's Heart 206
The Bliss Of Communion 207
　　　The Disciple To His Lord 207
　　　Joy In The Presence Of Jesus 208
　　　O Jesus, King Most Wonderful 209
　　　Christ Our Light 209
　　　As Ointment Poured Forth 210
　　　O! Tell Me, Thou Life And Delight Of My Soul! 211
　　　The Face Of Christ 212
　　　Christ, Whose Glory Fills The Skies 212

Jesu, Highest Heaven's Completeness 213
　　Show Me Thy Face 213
　　None Other Lamb, None Other Name 214
　　Aspirations Of The Soul After Christ 215
　　The Pain Of Love 216
　　Thou Hidden Source Of Calm Repose 217
　　The Man Divine 218
　　Thee Will I Love 219
　　At The Lord's Table 221
　　Prayer Before Communion 222
　　The Indwelling Christ 222
　　As Incense Streaming Forth 223
　　Hosanna, Lord! 224
　　Am I Not Enough? 225
　　Jesus, Thou Joy Of Loving Hearts 225

Joyous Anticipation Of Christ's Return 227
　　Wake, Awake, For Night Is Flying 227
　　Lo! He Comes! 228
　　The Hope Of His Coming 230
　　The Blessed Morrow 230

Immortality And The World To Come 232
　　Lift Your Glad Voices 232
　　Jesus Lives, And So Shall I 232
　　O Sing Hallelujah! 234
　　Those Endless Sabbaths 235
　　In Immanuel's Land 235
　　The Celestial Country 240

Notes 252

Foreword

In the four works collected here, A.W. Tozer exhorts the faithful to develop a deeper understanding of God and a closer relationship with Him. Through prayer, meditation, study, and a close adherence to the scriptures, Tozer shows that a powerful spiritual life is available to all who seek it.

A.W. Tozer (1897-1963) spent his career as a pastor with the Christian and Missionary Alliance. He received no formal education after his youth, instead working as a laborer. Coming home one day as a teen, he heard a street preacher say, "If you don't know how to be saved...just call on God, saying 'Lord be merciful to me a sinner.'" This call began a life devoted to Christ.

Tozer began a course of self-education, reading and studying the Bible and other works by Christian thinkers. By the age of twenty-two, he became pastor of his first church. Throughout his career, he served as a spiritual leader to his small congregations. He also became a well-loved Christian writer, publishing books and articles for magazines like *Christian Life* and *Alliance Weekly*.

Throughout all his writings, Tozer focused on the fundamentals of Christianity, always supported by the scriptures. He consistently eschewed complexity. Instead, he always returned to simple prayer and worship as the path to God.

The Pursuit of God is one of Tozer's best-loved books. Considered a Christian classic, it seeks to bridge the gap between an understanding of the Biblical fundamentals and the all-consuming feeling of a deeper Presence. Once a Christian begins to pursue God, Tozer says, he will find that God's love is in fact pursuing him right back.

Tozer felt that worldliness was one of the strongest barriers to a better connection with God. He urged readers to abandon their love of the material, and to meditate on the proper relationship of man to God. Each chapter contains a new lesson that can help the reader break down another barrier between himself and his Creator.

Keys to the Deeper Life includes four of Tozer's essays on the spiritual lives of his fellow Christians. He discourages the faithful from focusing on increasing the number of Christ's followers. First, there must be a return to "New Testament Christianity, not in creed only but in complete manner of life as well."

He had observed that his contemporaries were content with an average spiritual life, leaving so many of God's gifts unearned through their complacency. Tozer hoped to awaken his readers to the possibility of a stronger faith and deeper relationship with God.

How to Be Filled with the Holy Spirit is a collection of four of Tozer's sermons that explore the nature of the third element of the Holy Trinity. The Spirit is not a What, but a Who—a Person without matter who permeates everything around us. Tozer asks the reader to dive deep within themselves to ask if they truly want to be filled with the Holy Spirit. For to do so, the faithful must surrender themselves completely to the will of God.

Originally written as sermons to be spoken rather than read, this collection has a simple conversational style that readers will find approachable. Tozer explores a complicated, abstract concept and turns it into something the reader can comprehend and internalize.

The Christian Book of Mystical Verse is a collection of hymns, verses, and poetry curated by Tozer. Written by Christians of many different denominations and nationalities, each contribution "...begin[s] with God, embrace[s] the worshipping soul and return[s] to God again." Tozer organized the verses into fifteen categories to be used as a daily devotional, or as a guide when the reader wishes to pray on a specific topic.

Tozer's writing gets to the heart of Biblical truth. His call to "...follow your Lord and pay no heed to the passing religious vogue," provides a guiding light amid the distractions of modern life.

The Pursuit of God

[1948]

INTRODUCTION

Here is a masterly study of the inner life by a heart thirsting after God, eager to grasp at least the outskirts of His ways, the abyss of His love for sinners, and the height of His unapproachable majesty—and it was written by a busy pastor in Chicago!

Who could imagine David writing the twenty-third Psalm on South Halsted Street, or a medieval mystic finding inspiration in a small study on the second floor of a frame house on that vast, flat checkerboard of endless streets.

> *Where cross the crowded ways of life*
> *Where sound the cries of race and clan,*
> *In haunts of wretchedness and need,*
> *On shadowed threshold dark with fears,*
> *And paths where hide the lures of greed...*

But even as Dr. Frank Mason North, of New York, says in his immortal poem, so Mr. Tozer says in this book:

> *Above the noise of selfish strife*
> *We hear Thy voice, O Son of Man.*

My acquaintance with the author is limited to brief visits and loving fellowship in his church. There I discovered a self-made scholar, an omnivorous reader with a remarkable library of theological and devotional books, and one who seemed to burn the midnight oil in pursuit of God. His book is the result of long meditation and much prayer. It is not a collection of sermons. It does not deal with the pulpit and the pew but with the soul athirst for God. The chapters could be summarized in Moses' prayer, "Show me thy glory," or Paul's exclamation, "O the depth of the riches both of the wisdom and knowledge of God!" It is theology not of the head but of the heart.

There is deep insight, sobriety of style, and a catholicity of outlook that is refreshing. The author has few quotations but he knows the saints and mystics of the centuries—Augustine, Nicholas of Cusa, Thomas a Kempis, von Hugel, Finney, Wesley and many more. The ten chapters are heart searching and the prayers at the close of each are for closet, not pulpit. I felt the nearness of God while reading them.

Here is a book for every pastor, missionary, and devout Christian. It deals with the deep things of God and the riches of His grace. Above all, it has the keynote of sincerity and humility.

Samuel M. Zwemer
New York City

Preface

In this hour of all-but-universal darkness one cheering gleam appears: within the fold of conservative Christianity there are to be found increasing numbers of persons whose religious lives are marked by a growing hunger after God Himself. They are eager for spiritual realities and will not be put off with words, nor will they be content with correct "interpretations" of truth. They are athirst for God, and they will not be satisfied till they have drunk deep at the Fountain of Living Water.

This is the only real harbinger of revival which I have been able to detect anywhere on the religious horizon. It may be the cloud the size of a man's hand for which a few saints here and there have been looking. It can result in a resurrection of life for many souls and a recapture of that radiant wonder which should accompany faith in Christ, that wonder which has all but fled the Church of God in our day.

But this hunger must be recognized by our religious leaders. Current evangelicalism has (to change the figure) laid the altar and divided the sacrifice into parts, but now seems satisfied to count the stones and rearrange the pieces with never a care that there is not a sign of fire upon the top of lofty Carmel. But God be thanked that there are a few who care. They are those who, while they love the altar and delight in the sacrifice, are yet unable to reconcile themselves to the continued absence of fire. They desire God above all. They are athirst to taste for themselves the "piercing sweetness" of the love of Christ about Whom all the holy prophets did write and the psalmists did sing.

There is today no lack of Bible teachers to set forth correctly the principles of the doctrines of Christ, but too many of these seem satisfied to teach the fundamentals of the faith year after year, strangely unaware that there is in their ministry no manifest Presence, nor anything unusual in their personal lives. They minister constantly to believers who feel within their breasts a longing which their teaching simply does not satisfy.

I trust I speak in charity, but the lack in our pulpits is real. Milton's terrible sentence applies to our day as accurately as it did to his: "The hungry sheep look up, and are not fed." It is a solemn thing, and no small scandal in the Kingdom, to see God's children starving while actually seated at the Father's table. The truth of Wesley's words is established before our eyes: "Orthodoxy, or right opinion, is, at best, a very slender part of religion. Though right tempers cannot subsist without right opinions, yet right opinions may subsist without right tempers. There may be a right opinion of God without either love or one right temper toward Him. Satan is a proof of this."

Thanks to our splendid Bible societies and to other effective agencies for the dissemination of the Word, there are today many millions of people who hold "right opinions," probably more than ever before in the history of the Church. Yet I wonder if there was ever a time when true spiritual worship was at a lower ebb. To great sections of the Church the art of worship has been lost entirely, and in its place has come that strange and foreign thing called the "program." This word has been borrowed from the stage and applied with sad wisdom to the type of public service which new passes for worship among us.

Sound Bible exposition is an imperative must in the Church of the Living God. Without it no church can be a New Testament church in any strict meaning of that term. But exposition may be carried on in such way as to leave the hearers devoid of any true spiritual nourishment whatever. For it is not mere words that nourish the soul, but God Himself, and unless and until the hearers find God in personal experience they are not the better for having heard the truth. The Bible is not an end in itself, but a means to bring men to an intimate and satisfying knowledge of God, that they may enter into Him, that they may delight in His Presence, may taste and know the inner sweetness of the very God Himself in the core and center of their hearts.

This book is a modest attempt to aid God's hungry children so to find Him. Nothing here is new except in the sense that it is a discovery which my own heart has made of spiritual realities most delightful and wonderful to me. Others before me have gone much farther into these holy mysteries than I have done, but if my fire is not large it is yet real, and there may be those who can light their candle at its flame.

A. W. Tozer
Chicago, Ill.
June 16, 1948

FOLLOWING HARD AFTER GOD

*My soul followeth hard after thee:
thy right hand upholdeth me.—Psa. 63:8*

Christian theology teaches the doctrine of prevenient grace, which briefly stated means this, that before a man can seek God, God must first have sought the man.

Before a sinful man can think a right thought of God, there must have been a work of enlightenment done within him; imperfect it may be, but a true work nonetheless, and the secret cause of all desiring and seeking and praying which may follow.

We pursue God because, and only because, He has first put an urge within us that spurs us to the pursuit. "No man can come to me," said our Lord, "except the Father which hath sent me draw him," and it is by this very prevenient drawing that God takes from us every vestige of credit for the act of coming. The impulse to pursue God originates with God, but the outworking of that impulse is our following hard after Him; and all the time we are pursuing Him we are already in His hand: "Thy right hand upholdeth me."

In this divine "upholding" and human "following" there is no contradiction. All is of God, for as von Hugel teaches, God is always previous. In practice, however, (that is, where God's previous working meets man's present response) man must pursue God. On our part there must be positive reciprocation if this secret drawing of God is to eventuate in identifiable experience of the Divine. In the warm language of personal feeling this is stated in the Forty-second Psalm: "As the hart panteth after the water brooks, so panteth my soul after thee. O God. My soul thirst-eth for God, for the living God: when shall I come and appear before God?" This is deep calling unto deep, and the longing heart will understand it.

The doctrine of justification by faith—a Biblical truth, and a blessed relief from sterile legalism and unavailing self-effort—has in our time fallen into evil company and been interpreted by many in such manner as actually to bar men from the knowledge of God. The whole transaction of religious conversion has been made mechanical and spiritless. Faith may now be exercised without a jar to the moral life and without embarrassment to the Adamic ego. Christ may be "received" without creating any special love for Him in the soul of the receiver. The man is "saved," but he is not hungry nor thirsty after God. In fact he is specifically taught to be satisfied and encouraged to be content with little.

The modern scientist has lost God amid the wonders of His world; we Christians are in real danger of losing God amid the wonders of His Word. We have almost forgotten that God is a Person and, as such, can be cultivated as any person can. It is inherent in personality to be able to know other personalities, but full knowledge of one personality by another cannot be achieved in one encounter. It is only after long and loving mental intercourse that the full possibilities of both can be explored.

All social intercourse between human beings is a response of personality to personality, grading upward from the most casual brush between man and man to the fullest, most intimate communion of which the human soul is capable. Religion, so far as it is genuine, is in essence the response of created personalities to the Creating Personality, God. "This is life eternal, that they might know thee the only true God, and Jesus Christ, whom thou hast sent."

God is a Person, and in the deep of His mighty nature He thinks, wills, enjoys, feels, loves, desires and suffers as any other person may. In making Himself known to us He stays by the familiar pattern of personality. He communicates with us through the avenues of our minds, our wills and our emotions. The continuous and unembarrassed interchange of love and thought between God and the soul of the redeemed man is the throbbing heart of New Testament religion.

This intercourse between God and the soul is known to us in conscious personal awareness. It is personal: that is, it does not come through the body of believers, as such, but is known to the individual, and to the body through the individuals which compose it. And it is conscious: that is, it does not stay below the threshold of consciousness and work there unknown to the soul (as, for instance, infant baptism is thought by some to do), but comes within the field of awareness where the man can "know" it as he knows any other fact of experience.

You and I are in little (our sins excepted) what God is in large. Being made in His image we have within us the capacity to know Him. In our sins we lack only the power. The moment the Spirit has quickened us to life in regeneration our whole being senses its kinship to God and leaps up in joyous recognition. That is the heavenly birth without which we cannot see the Kingdom of God. It is, however, not an end but an inception, for now begins the glorious pursuit, the heart's happy exploration of the infinite riches of the Godhead. That is where we begin, I say, but where we stop no man has yet discovered, for there is in the awful and mysterious depths of the Triune God neither limit nor end.

> *Shoreless Ocean, who can sound Thee?*
> *Thine own eternity is round Thee,*
> *Majesty divine!*

To have found God and still to pursue Him is the soul's paradox of love, scorned indeed by the too-easily-satisfied religionist, but justified in happy experience by the children of the burning heart. St. Bernard stated this holy paradox in a musical quatrain that will be instantly understood by every worshipping soul:

> *We taste Thee, O Thou Living Bread,*
> *And long to feast upon Thee still:*
> *We drink of Thee, the Fountainhead*
> *And thirst our souls from Thee to fill.*

Come near to the holy men and women of the past and you will soon feel the heat of their desire after God. They mourned for Him, they prayed and wrestled and sought for Him day and night, in season and out, and when they had found Him the finding was all the sweeter for the long seeking. Moses used the fact that he knew God as an argument for knowing Him better. "Now, therefore, I pray thee, if I have found grace in thy sight, show me now thy way, that I may know thee, that I may find grace in thy sight"; and from there he rose to make the daring request, "I beseech thee, show me thy glory." God was frankly pleased by this display of ardor, and the next day called Moses into the mount, and there in solemn procession made all His glory pass before him.

David's life was a torrent of spiritual desire, and his psalms ring with the cry of the seeker and the glad shout of the finder. Paul confessed the mainspring of his life to be his burning desire after Christ. "That I may know Him," was the goal of his heart, and to this he sacrificed everything. "Yea doubtless, and I count all things but loss for the excellency of the knowledge of Christ Jesus my Lord: for whom I have suffered the loss of all things, and do count them but refuse, that I may win Christ."

Hymnody is sweet with the longing after God, the God whom, while the singer seeks, he knows he has already found. "His track I see and

I'll pursue," sang our fathers only a short generation ago, but that song is heard no more in the great congregation. How tragic that we in this dark day have had our seeking done for us by our teachers. Everything is made to center upon the initial act of "accepting" Christ (a term, incidentally, which is not found in the Bible) and we are not expected thereafter to crave any further revelation of God to our souls. We have been snared in the coils of a spurious logic which insists that if we have found Him we need no more seek Him. This is set before us as the last word in orthodoxy, and it is taken for granted that no Bible-taught Christian ever believed otherwise. Thus the whole testimony of the worshipping, seeking, singing Church on that subject is crisply set aside. The experiential heart-theology of a grand army of fragrant saints is rejected in favor of a smug interpretation of Scripture which would certainly have sounded strange to an Augustine, a Rutherford or a Brainerd.

In the midst of this great chill there are some, I rejoice to acknowledge, who will not be content with shallow logic. They will admit the force of the argument, and then turn away with tears to hunt some lonely place and pray, "O God, show me thy glory." They want to taste, to touch with their hearts, to see with their inner eyes the wonder that is God.

I want deliberately to encourage this mighty longing after God. The lack of it has brought us to our present low estate. The stiff and wooden quality about our religious lives is a result of our lack of holy desire. Complacency is a deadly foe of all spiritual growth. Acute desire must be present or there will be no manifestation of Christ to His people. He waits to be wanted. Too bad that with many of us He waits so long, so very long, in vain.

Every age has its own characteristics. Right now we are in an age of religious complexity. The simplicity which is in Christ is rarely found among us. In its stead are programs, methods, organizations and a world of nervous activities which occupy time and attention but can never satisfy the longing of the heart. The shallowness of our inner experience, the hollowness of our worship, and that servile imitation of the world which marks our promotional methods all testify that we, in this day, know God only imperfectly, and the peace of God scarcely at all.

If we would find God amid all the religious externals we must first determine to find Him, and then proceed in the way of simplicity. Now as always God discovers Himself to "babes" and hides Himself in thick darkness from the wise and the prudent. We must simplify our approach to Him. We must strip down to essentials (and they will be found to be blessedly few). We must put away all effort to impress, and come with the guileless candor of childhood. If we do this, without doubt God will quickly respond.

When religion has said its last word, there is little that we need other than God Himself. The evil habit of seeking God-and effectively prevents us from finding God in full revelation. In the "and" lies our great woe. If we omit the "and" we shall soon find God, and in Him we shall find that for which we have all our lives been secretly longing.

We need not fear that in seeking God only we may narrow our lives or restrict the motions of our expanding hearts. The opposite is true. We can well afford to make God our All, to concentrate, to sacrifice the many for the One.

The author of the quaint old English classic, The Cloud of Unknowing, teaches us how to do this. "Lift up thine heart unto God with a meek stirring of love; and mean Himself, and none of His goods. And thereto, look thee loath to think on aught but God Himself. So that nought work in thy wit, nor in thy will, but only God Himself. This is the work of the soul that most pleaseth God."

Again, he recommends that in prayer we practice a further stripping down of everything, even of our theology. "For it sufficeth enough, a naked intent direct unto God without any other cause than Himself." Yet underneath all his thinking lay the broad foundation of New Testament truth, for he explains that by "Himself" he means "God that made thee, and bought thee, and that graciously called thee to thy degree." And he is all for simplicity: If we would have religion "lapped and folden in one word, for that thou shouldst have better hold thereupon, take thee but a little word of one syllable: for so it is better than of two, for even the shorter it is the better it accordeth with the work of the Spirit. And such a word is this word GOD or this word LOVE."

When the Lord divided Canaan among the tribes of Israel Levi received no share of the land. God said to him simply, "I am thy part and thine inheritance," and by those words made him richer than all his brethren, richer than all the kings and rajas who have ever lived in the world. And there is a spiritual principle here, a principle still valid for every priest of the Most High God.

The man who has God for his treasure has all things in One. Many ordinary treasures may be denied him, or if he is allowed to have them, the enjoyment of them will be so tempered that they will never be necessary to his happiness. Or if he must see them go, one after one, he will scarcely feel a sense of loss, for having the Source of all things he has in One all satisfaction, all pleasure, all delight. Whatever he may lose he has actually lost nothing, for he now has it all in One, and he has it purely, legitimately and forever.

O God, I have tasted Thy goodness, and it has both satisfied me and made me thirsty for more. I am painfully conscious of my need of further grace. I am ashamed of my lack of desire. O God, the Triune God, I want to want Thee; I long to be filled with longing; I thirst to be made more thirsty still. Show me Thy glory, I pray Thee, that so I may know Thee indeed. Begin in mercy a new work of love within me. Say to my soul, "Rise up, my love, my fair one, and come away." Then give me grace to rise and follow Thee up from this misty lowland where I have wandered so long. In Jesus' Name, Amen.

The Blessedness of Possessing Nothing

*Blessed are the poor in spirit:
for theirs is the kindgom of heaven.—Matt. 5:3*

Before the Lord God made man upon the earth He first prepared for him by creating a world of useful and pleasant things for his sustenance and delight. In the Genesis account of the creation these are called simply "things." They were made for man's uses, but they were meant always to be external to the man and subservient to him. In the deep heart of the man was a shrine where none but God was worthy to come. Within him was God; without, a thousand gifts which God had showered upon him.

But sin has introduced complications and has made those very gifts of God a potential source of ruin to the soul.

Our woes began when God was forced out of His central shrine and "things" were allowed to enter.

Within the human heart "things" have taken over. Men have now by nature no peace within their hearts, for God is crowned there no longer, but there in the moral dusk stubborn and aggressive usurpers fight among themselves for first place on the throne.

This is not a mere metaphor, but an accurate analysis of our real spiritual trouble. There is within the human heart a tough fibrous root of fallen life whose nature is to possess, always to possess. It covets "things" with a deep and fierce passion. The pronouns "my" and "mine" look innocent enough in print, but their constant and universal use is significant. They express the real nature of the old Adamic man better than a thousand volumes of theology could do. They are verbal symptoms of our deep disease. The roots of our hearts have grown down into things, and we dare not pull up one rootlet lest we die. Things have become necessary to us, a development never originally intended. God's gifts now take the place of God, and the whole course of nature is upset by the monstrous substitution.

Our Lord referred to this tyranny of things when He said to His disciples, "If any man will come after me, let him deny himself, and take up his cross, and follow me. For whosoever will save his life shall lose it: and whosoever shall lose his life for my sake shall find it."

Breaking this truth into fragments for our better understanding, it would seem that there is within each of us an enemy which we tolerate at our peril. Jesus called it "life" and "self," or as we would say, the self-life. Its chief characteristic is its possessiveness: the words "gain" and "profit" suggest this. To allow this enemy to live is in the end to lose everything. To repudiate it and give up all for Christ's sake is to lose nothing at last, but to preserve everything unto life eternal. And possibly also a hint is given here as to the only effective way to destroy this foe: it is by the Cross. "Let him take up his cross and follow me."

The way to deeper knowledge of God is through the lonely valleys of soul poverty and abnegation of all things. The blessed ones who possess the Kingdom are they who have repudiated every external thing and have rooted from their hearts all sense of possessing. These are the "poor in spirit." They have reached an inward state paralleling the outward circumstances of the common beggar in the streets of Jerusalem; that is what the word "poor" as Christ used it actually means. These blessed poor are no longer slaves to the tyranny of things. They have broken the yoke of the oppressor; and this they have done not by fighting but by surrendering. Though free from all sense of possessing, they yet possess all things. "Theirs is the kingdom of heaven."

Let me exhort you to take this seriously. It is not to be understood as mere Bible teaching to be stored away in the mind along with an inert mass of other doctrines. It is a marker on the road to greener pastures, a path chiseled against the steep sides of the mount of God. We dare not try to by-pass it if we would follow on in this holy pursuit. We must ascend a step at a time. If we refuse one step we bring our progress to an end.

As is frequently true, this New Testament principle of spiritual life finds its best illustration in the Old Testament. In the story of Abraham and Isaac we have a dramatic picture of the surrendered life as well as an excellent commentary on the first Beatitude.

Abraham was old when Isaac was born, old enough indeed to have been his grandfather, and the child became at once the delight and idol of his heart. From that moment when he first stooped to take the tiny form awkwardly in his arms he was an eager love slave of his son. God went out of His way to comment on the strength of this affection. And it is not hard to understand. The baby represented everything sacred to his father's heart: the promises of God, the covenants, the hopes of the years and the long messianic dream. As he watched him grow from babyhood to young manhood the heart of the old man was knit closer and closer with the life of his son, till at last the relationship bordered upon the perilous. It was then that God stepped in to save both father and son from the consequences of an uncleansed love.

"Take now thy son," said God to Abraham, "thine only son Isaac, whom thou lovest, and get thee into the land of Moriah; and offer him there for a burnt-offering upon one of the mountains which I will tell thee of." The sacred writer spares us a close-up of the agony that night on the slopes near Beersheba when the aged man had it out with his God, but respectful imagination may view in awe the bent form and convulsive wrestling alone under the stars. Possibly not again until a Greater than Abraham wrestled in the Garden of Gethsemane did such mortal pain visit a human soul. If only the man himself might have been allowed to die. That would have been easier a thousand times, for he was old now, and to die would have been no great ordeal for one who had walked so long with God. Besides, it would have been a last sweet pleasure to let his dimming vision rest upon the figure of his stalwart son who would live to carry on the Abrahamic line and fulfill in himself the promises of God made long before in Ur of the Chaldees.

How should he slay the lad! Even if he could get the consent of his wounded and protesting heart, how could he reconcile the act with the promise, "In Isaac shall thy seed be called"? This was Abraham's trial by fire, and he did not fail in the crucible. While the stars still shone like sharp white points above the tent where the sleeping Isaac lay, and long before the gray dawn had begun to lighten the east, the old saint had made up his mind. He would offer his son as God had directed him to do, and then trust God to raise him from the dead. This, says the writer to the Hebrews, was the solution his aching heart found sometime in the dark night, and he rose "early in the morning" to carry out the plan. It is beautiful to see that, while he erred as to God's method, he had correctly sensed the secret of His great heart. And the solution accords well with the New Testament Scripture, "Whosoever will lose for my sake shall find."

God let the suffering old man go through with it up to the point where He knew there would be no retreat, and then forbade him to lay a hand upon the boy. To the wondering patriarch He now says in effect, "It's all right, Abraham. I never intended that you should actually slay the lad. I only wanted to remove him from the temple of your heart that I might reign unchallenged there. I wanted to correct the perversion that existed in your love. Now you may have the boy, sound and well. Take him and go back to your tent. Now I know that thou fearest God, seeing that thou hast not withheld thy son, thine only son, from me."

Then heaven opened and a voice was heard saying to him, "By myself have I sworn, saith the Lord, for because thou hast done this thing, and hast not withheld thy son, thine only son: that in blessing I will bless thee, and in multiplying I will multiply thy seed as the stars of the heaven, and as the sand which is upon the sea shore; and thy seed shall possess the gate of his enemies; and in thy seed shall all the nations of the earth be blessed; because thou hast obeyed my voice."

The old man of God lifted his head to respond to the Voice, and stood there on the mount strong and pure and grand, a man marked out by the Lord for special treatment, a friend and favorite of the Most High. Now he was a man wholly surrendered, a man utterly obedient, a man who possessed nothing. He had concentrated his all in the person of his dear son, and God had taken it from him. God could have begun out on the margin of Abraham's life and worked inward to the center; He chose rather to cut quickly to the heart and have it over in one sharp act of separation. In dealing thus He practiced an economy of means and time. It hurt cruelly, but it was effective.

I have said that Abraham possessed nothing. Yet was not this poor man rich? Everything he had owned before was his still to enjoy: sheep, camels, herds, and goods of every sort. He had also his wife and his friends, and best of all he had his son Isaac safe by his side. He had everything, but he possessed nothing. There is the spiritual secret. There is the sweet theology of the heart which can be learned only in the school of renunciation. The books on systematic theology overlook this, but the wise will understand.

After that bitter and blessed experience I think the words "my" and "mine" never had again the same meaning for Abraham. The sense of possession which they connote was gone from his heart. Things had been cast out forever. They had now become external to the man. His inner heart was free from them. The world said, "Abraham is rich," but the aged patriarch only smiled. He could not explain it to them, but he knew that he owned nothing, that his real treasures were inward and eternal.

There can be no doubt that this possessive clinging to things is one of the most harmful habits in the life. Because it is so natural it is rarely recognized for the evil that it is; but its outworkings are tragic.

We are often hindered from giving up our treasures to the Lord out of fear for their safety; this is especially true when those treasures are loved relatives and friends. But we need have no such fears. Our Lord came not to destroy but to save. Everything is safe which we commit to Him, and nothing is really safe which is not so committed.

Our gifts and talents should also be turned over to Him. They should be recognized for what they are, God's loan to us, and should never be considered in any sense our own. We have no more right to claim credit for special abilities than for blue eyes or strong muscles. "For who maketh thee to differ from another? and what hast thou that thou didst not receive?"

The Christian who is alive enough to know himself even slightly will recognize the symptoms of this possession malady, and will grieve to find them in his own heart. If the longing after God is strong enough within him he will want to do something about the matter. Now, what should he do?

First of all he should put away all defense and make no attempt to excuse himself either in his own eyes or before the Lord. Whoever defends himself will have himself for his defense, and he will have no other; but let him come defenseless before the Lord and he will have for his defender no less than God Himself. Let the inquiring Christian trample under foot every slippery trick of his deceitful heart and insist upon frank and open relations with the Lord.

Then he should remember that this is holy business. No careless or casual dealings will suffice. Let him come to God in full determination to be heard. Let him insist that God accept his all, that He take things out of his heart and Himself reign there in power. It may be he will need to become specific, to name things and people by their names one by one. If he will become drastic enough he can shorten the time of his travail from years to minutes and enter the good land long before his slower brethren who coddle their feelings and insist upon caution in their dealings with God.

Let us never forget that such a truth as this cannot be learned by rote as one would learn the facts of physical science. They must be experienced before we can really know them. We must in our hearts live through Abraham's harsh and bitter experiences if we would know the blessedness which follows them. The ancient curse will not go out painlessly; the tough old miser within us will not lie down and die obedient to our command. He must be torn out of our heart like a plant from the soil; he must be extracted in agony and blood like a tooth from the jaw. He must be expelled from our soul by violence as Christ expelled the money changers from the temple. And we shall need to steel ourselves against his piteous begging, and to recognize it as springing out of self-pity, one of the most reprehensible sins of the human heart.

If we would indeed know God in growing intimacy, we must go this way of renunciation. And if we are set upon the pursuit of God He will sooner or later bring us to this test. Abraham's testing was, at the time, not known to him as such, yet if he had taken some course other than the one he did, the whole history of the Old Testament would have been different. God would have found His man, no doubt, but the loss to Abraham would have been tragic beyond the telling. So we will be brought one by one to the testing place, and we may never know when we are there. At that testing place there will be no dozen possible choices for us; just one and an alternative, but our whole future will be conditioned by the choice we make.

Father, I want to know Thee, but my coward heart fears to give up its toys. I cannot part with them without inward bleeding, and I do not try to hide from Thee the terror of the parting. I come trembling, but I do come. Please root from my heart all those things which I have cherished so long and which have become a very part of my living self, so that Thou mayest enter and dwell there without a rival. Then shalt Thou make the place of Thy feet glorious. Then shall my heart have no need of the sun to shine in it, for Thyself wilt be the light of it, and there shall be no night there. In Jesus' Name, Amen.

Removing the Veil

*Having therefore, brethren, boldness
to enter into the holiest by the blood
of Jesus. — Heb. 10:19*

Among the famous sayings of the Church fathers none is better known than Augustine's, "Thou hast formed us for Thyself, and our hearts are restless till they find rest in Thee."

The great saint states here in few words the origin and interior history of the human race. God made us for Himself: that is the only explanation that satisfies the heart of a thinking man, whatever his wild reason may say. Should faulty education and perverse reasoning lead a man to conclude otherwise, there is little that any Christian can do for him. For such a man I have no message. My appeal is addressed to those who have been previously taught in secret by the wisdom of God; I speak to thirsty hearts whose longings have been wakened by the touch of God within them, and such as they need no reasoned proof. Their restless hearts furnish all the proof they need.

God formed us for Himself. The Shorter Catechism, "Agreed upon by the Reverend Assembly of Divines at Westminster," as the old New-England Primer has it, asks the ancient questions what and why and answers them in one short sentence hardly matched in any uninspired work. "Question: What is the chief End of Man? Answer: Man's chief End is to glorify God and enjoy Him forever." With this agree the four and twenty elders who fall on their faces to worship Him that liveth for ever and ever, saying, "Thou art worthy, O Lord, to receive glory and honour and power: for thou hast created all things, and for thy pleasure they are and were created."

God formed us for His pleasure, and so formed us that we as well as He can in divine communion enjoy the sweet and mysterious mingling of kindred personalities. He meant us to see Him and live with Him and draw our life from His smile. But we have been guilty of that "foul revolt" of which Milton speaks when describing the rebellion of Satan and his hosts. We have broken with God. We have ceased to obey Him or love Him and in guilt and fear have fled as far as possible from His Presence.

Yet who can flee from His Presence when the heaven and the heaven of heavens cannot contain Him? when as the wisdom of Solomon testifies, "the Spirit of the Lord filleth the world?" The omnipresence of the Lord is one thing, and is a solemn fact necessary to His perfection; the manifest Presence is another thing altogether, and from that Presence we have fled, like Adam, to hide among the trees of the garden, or like Peter to shrink away crying, "Depart from me, for I am a sinful man, O Lord."

So the life of man upon the earth is a life away from the Presence, wrenched loose from that "blissful center" which is our right and proper dwelling place, our first estate which we kept not, the loss of which is the cause of our unceasing restlessness.

The whole work of God in redemption is to undo the tragic effects of that foul revolt, and to bring us back again into right and eternal relationship with Himself. This required that our sins be disposed of satisfactorily, that a full reconciliation be effected and the way opened for us to return again into conscious communion with God and to live again in the Presence as before. Then by His prevenient working within us He moves us to return. This first comes to our notice when our restless hearts feel a yearning for the Presence of God and we say within ourselves, "I will arise and go to my Father." That is the first step, and as the Chinese sage Lao-tze has said, "The journey of a thousand miles begins with a first step."

The interior journey of the soul from the wilds of sin into the enjoyed Presence of God is beautifully illustrated in the Old Testament tabernacle. The returning sinner first entered the outer court where he offered a blood sacrifice on the brazen altar and washed himself in the laver that stood near it. Then through a veil he passed into the holy place where no natural light could come, but the golden candlestick which spoke of Jesus the Light of the World threw its soft glow over all. There also was the shewbread to tell of Jesus, the Bread of Life, and the altar of incense, a figure of unceasing prayer.

Though the worshipper had enjoyed so much, still he had not yet entered the Presence of God. Another veil separated from the Holy of Holies where above the mercy seat dwelt the very God Himself in awful and glorious manifestation. While the tabernacle stood, only the high priest could enter there, and that but once a year, with blood which he offered for his sins and the sins of the people. It was this last veil which was rent when our Lord gave up the ghost on Calvary, and the sacred writer explains that this rending of the veil opened the way for every worshipper in the world to come by the new and living way straight into the divine Presence.

Everything in the New Testament accords with this Old Testament picture. Ransomed men need no longer pause in fear to enter the Holy of Holies. God wills that we should push on into His Presence and live our whole life there. This is to be known to us in conscious experience. It is more than a doctrine to be held, it is a life to be enjoyed every moment of every day.

This Flame of the Presence was the beating heart of the Levitical order. Without it all the appointments of the tabernacle were characters of some unknown language; they had no meaning for Israel or for us. The greatest fact of the tabernacle was that Jehovah was there; a Presence was waiting within the veil. Similarly the Presence of God is the central fact of Christianity. At the heart of the Christian message is God Himself waiting for His redeemed children to push in to conscious awareness of His Presence. That type of Christianity which happens now to be the vogue knows this Presence only in theory. It fails to stress the Christian's privilege of present realization. According to its teachings we are in the Presence of God positionally, and nothing is said about the need to experience that Presence actually. The fiery urge that drove men like McCheyne is wholly missing. And the present generation of Christians measures itself by this imperfect rule. Ignoble contentment takes the place of burning zeal. We are satisfied to rest in our judicial possessions and for the most part we bother ourselves very little about the absence of personal experience.

Who is this within the veil who dwells in fiery manifestations? It is none other than God Himself, "One God the Father Almighty, Maker of heaven and earth, and of all things visible and invisible," and "One Lord Jesus Christ, the only begotten Son of God; begotten of His Father before all worlds, God of God, Light of Light, Very God of Very God; begotten, not made; being of one substance with the Father," and "the Holy Ghost, the Lord and Giver of life, Who proceedeth from the Father and the Son, Who with the Father and the Son together is worshipped and glorified." Yet this holy Trinity is One God, for "we worship one God in Trinity, and Trinity in Unity; neither confounding the Persons, nor dividing the Substance. For there is one Person of the Father, another of the Son, and another of the Holy Ghost. But the Godhead of the Father, of the Son, and of the Holy Ghost, is all one: the glory equal and the majesty co-eternal." So in part run the ancient creeds, and so the inspired Word declares.

Behind the veil is God, that God after Whom the world, with strange inconsistency, has felt, "if haply they might find Him." He has discovered

Himself to some extent in nature, but more perfectly in the Incarnation; now He waits to show Himself in ravishing fulness to the humble of soul and the pure in heart.

The world is perishing for lack of the knowledge of God and the Church is famishing for want of His Presence. The instant cure of most of our religious ills would be to enter the Presence in spiritual experience, to become suddenly aware that we are in God and that God is in us. This would lift us out of our pitiful narrowness and cause our hearts to be enlarged. This would burn away the impurities from our lives as the bugs and fungi were burned away by the fire that dwelt in the bush.

What a broad world to roam in, what a sea to swim in is this God and Father of our Lord Jesus Christ. He is eternal, which means that He antedates time and is wholly independent of it. Time began in Him and will end in Him. To it He pays no tribute and from it He suffers no change. He is immutable, which means that He has never changed and can never change in any smallest measure. To change He would need to go from better to worse or from worse to better. He cannot do either, for being perfect He cannot become more perfect, and if He were to become less perfect He would be less than God. He is omniscient, which means that He knows in one free and effortless act all matter, all spirit, all relationships, all events. He has no past and He has no future. He is, and none of the limiting and qualifying terms used of creatures can apply to Him. Love and mercy and righteousness are His, and holiness so ineffable that no comparisons or figures will avail to express it. Only fire can give even a remote conception of it. In fire He appeared at the burning bush; in the pillar of fire He dwelt through all the long wilderness journey. The fire that glowed between the wings of the cherubim in the holy place was called the "shekinah," the Presence, through the years of Israel's glory, and when the Old had given place to the New, He came at Pentecost as a fiery flame and rested upon each disciple.

Spinoza wrote of the intellectual love of God, and he had a measure of truth there; but the highest love of God is not intellectual, it is spiritual. God is spirit and only the spirit of man can know Him really. In the deep spirit of a man the fire must glow or his love is not the true love of God. The great of the Kingdom have been those who loved God more than others did. We all know who they have been and gladly pay tribute to the depths and sincerity of their devotion. We have but to pause for a moment and their names come trooping past us smelling of myrrh and aloes and cassia out of the ivory palaces.

Frederick Faber was one whose soul panted after God as the roe pants after the water brook, and the measure in which God revealed Himself to his seeking heart set the good man's whole life afire with a burning adoration rivaling that of the seraphim before the throne. His love for God extended to the three Persons of the Godhead equally, yet he seemed to feel for each One a special kind of love reserved for Him alone. Of God the Father he sings:

> *Only to sit and think, of God,*
> *Oh what a joy it is!*
> *To think the thought, to breathe the Name;*
> *Earth has no higher bliss.*
> *Father of Jesus, love's reward!*
> *What rapture will it be,*
> *Prostrate before Thy throne to lie,*
> *And gaze and gaze on Thee!*

His love for the Person of Christ was so intense that it threatened to consume him; it burned within him as a sweet and holy madness and flowed from his lips like molten gold. In one of his sermons he says, "Wherever we turn in the church of God, there is Jesus. He is the beginning, middle and end of everything to us. . . . There is nothing good, nothing holy, nothing beautiful, nothing joyous which He is not to His servants. No one need be poor, because, if he chooses, he can have Jesus for his own property and possession. No one need be downcast, for Jesus is the joy of heaven, and it is His joy to enter into sorrowful hearts. We can exaggerate about many things; but we can never exaggerate our obligation to Jesus, or the compassionate abundance of the love of Jesus to us. All our lives long we might talk of Jesus, and yet we should never come to an end of the sweet things that might be said of Him. Eternity will not be long enough to learn all He is, or to praise Him for all He has done, but then, that matters not; for we shall be always with Him, and we desire nothing more." And addressing our Lord directly he says to Him:

> *I love Thee so, I know not how*
> *My transports to control;*
> *Thy love is like a burning fire*
> *Within my very soul.*

Faber's blazing love extended also to the Holy Spirit. Not only in his theology did he acknowledge His deity and full equality with the Father and the Son, but he celebrated it constantly in his songs and in his prayers. He literally pressed his forehead to the ground in his eager fervid worship of the Third Person of the Godhead. In one of his great hymns to the Holy Spirit he sums up his burning devotion thus:

O Spirit, beautiful and dread!
My heart is fit to break
With love of all Thy tenderness
For us poor sinners' sake.

I have risked the tedium of quotation that I might show by pointed example what I have set out to say, viz., that God is so vastly wonderful, so utterly and completely delightful that He can, without anything other than Himself, meet and overflow the deepest demands of our total nature, mysterious and deep as that nature is. Such worship as Faber knew (and he is but one of a great company which no man can number) can never come from a mere doctrinal knowledge of God. Hearts that are "fit to break" with love for the Godhead are those who have been in the Presence and have looked with opened eye upon the majesty of Deity. Men of the breaking hearts had a quality about them not known to or understood by common men. They habitually spoke with spiritual authority. They had been in the Presence of God and they reported what they saw there. They were prophets, not scribes, for the scribe tells us what he has read, and the prophet tells what he has seen.

The distinction is not an imaginary one. Between the scribe who has read and the prophet who has seen there is a difference as wide as the sea. We are today overrun with orthodox scribes, but the prophets, where are they? The hard voice of the scribe sounds over evangelicalism, but the Church waits for the tender voice of the saint who has penetrated the veil and has gazed with inward eye upon the Wonder that is God. And yet, thus to penetrate, to push in sensitive living experience into the holy Presence, is a privilege open to every child of God.

With the veil removed by the rending of Jesus' flesh, with nothing on God's side to prevent us from entering, why do we tarry without? Why do we consent to abide all our days just outside the Holy of Holies and never enter at all to look upon God? We hear the Bridegroom say, "Let me see thy countenance, let me hear thy voice; for sweet is thy voice and thy countenance is comely." We sense that the call is for us, but still we fail to draw near, and the years pass and we grow old and tired in the outer courts of the tabernacle. What doth hinder us?

The answer usually given, simply that we are "cold," will not explain all the facts. There is something more serious than coldness of heart, something that may be back of that coldness and be the cause of its existence. What is it? What but the presence of a veil in our hearts? a veil not taken away as the first veil was, but which remains there still shutting out the light and hiding the face of God from us. It is the veil of our fleshly fallen nature living on, unjudged within us, uncrucified and unrepudiated. It is the close-woven veil of the self-life which we have never truly acknowledged, of which we have been secretly ashamed, and which for these reasons we have never brought to the judgment of the cross. It is not too mysterious, this opaque veil, nor is it hard to identify. We have but to look in our own hearts and we shall see it there, sewn and patched and repaired it may be, but there nevertheless, an enemy to our lives and an effective block to our spiritual progress.

This veil is not a beautiful thing and it is not a thing about which we commonly care to talk, but I am addressing the thirsting souls who are determined to follow God, and I know they will not turn back because the way leads temporarily through the blackened hills. The urge of God within them will assure their continuing the pursuit. They will face the facts however unpleasant and endure the cross for the joy set before them. So I am bold to name the threads out of which this inner veil is woven.

It is woven of the fine threads of the self-life, the hyphenated sins of the human spirit. They are not something we do, they are something we are, and therein lies both their subtlety and their power.

To be specific, the self-sins are these: self-righteousness, self-pity, self-confidence, self-sufficiency, self-admiration, self-love and a host of others like them. They dwell too deep within us and are too much a part of our natures to come to our attention till the light of God is focused upon them. The grosser manifestations of these sins, egotism, exhibitionism, self-promotion, are strangely tolerated in Christian leaders even in circles of impeccable orthodoxy. They are so much in evidence as actually, for many people, to become identified with the gospel. I trust it is not a cynical observation to say that they appear these days to be a requisite for popularity in some sections of the Church visible. Promoting self under the guise of promoting Christ is currently so common as to excite little notice.

One should suppose that proper instruction in the doctrines of man's depravity and the necessity for justification through the righteousness of Christ alone would deliver us from the power of the self-sins; but it does not work out that way. Self can live unrebuked at the very altar. It can watch the bleeding Victim die and not be in the least affected by what it sees. It can fight for the faith of the Reformers and preach eloquently the creed of salvation by grace, and gain strength by its efforts. To tell all the truth, it seems actually to feed upon orthodoxy and is more at home in a Bible Conference than in a tavern. Our very state of longing after God may afford it an excellent condition under which to thrive and grow.

Self is the opaque veil that hides the Face of God from us. It can be removed only in spiritual experience, never by mere instruction. As well try to instruct leprosy out of our system. There must be a work of God in destruction before we are free. We must invite the cross to do its deadly work within us. We must bring our self-sins to the cross for judgment. We must prepare ourselves for an ordeal of suffering in some measure like that through which our Saviour passed when He suffered under Pontius Pilate.

Let us remember: when we talk of the rending of the veil we are speaking in a figure, and the thought of it is poetical, almost pleasant; but in actuality there is nothing pleasant about it. In human experience that veil is made of living spiritual tissue; it is composed of the sentient, quivering stuff of which our whole beings consist, and to touch it is to touch us where we feel pain. To tear it away is to injure us, to hurt us and make us bleed. To say otherwise is to make the cross no cross and death no death at all. It is never fun to die. To rip through the dear and tender stuff of which life is made can never be anything but deeply painful. Yet that is what the cross did to Jesus and it is what the cross would do to every man to set him free.

Let us beware of tinkering with our inner life in hope ourselves to rend the veil. God must do everything for us. Our part is to yield and trust. We must confess, forsake, repudiate the self-life, and then reckon it crucified. But we must be careful to distinguish lazy "acceptance" from the real work of God. We must insist upon the work being done. We dare not rest content with a neat doctrine of self-crucifixion. That is to imitate Saul and spare the best of the sheep and the oxen.

Insist that the work be done in very truth and it will be done. The cross is rough, and it is deadly, but it is effective. It does not keep its victim hanging there forever. There comes a moment when its work is finished and the suffering victim dies. After that is resurrection glory and power, and the pain is forgotten for joy that the veil is taken away and we have entered in actual spiritual experience the Presence of the living God.

Lord, how excellent are Thy ways, and how devious and dark are the ways of man. Show us how to die, that we may rise again to newness of life. Rend the veil of our self-life from the top down as Thou didst rend the veil of the Temple. We would draw near in full assurance of faith. We would dwell with Thee in daily experience here on this earth so that we may be accustomed to the glory when we enter Thy heaven to dwell with Thee there. In Jesus' name, Amen.

APPREHENDING GOD

O taste and see.—Psa. 34:8

It was Canon Holmes, of India, who more than twenty-five years ago called attention to the inferential character of the average man's faith in God. To most people God is an inference, not a reality. He is a deduction from evidence which they consider adequate; but He remains personally unknown to the individual. "He must be," they say, "therefore we believe He is." Others do not go even so far as this; they know of Him only by hearsay. They have never bothered to think the matter out for themselves, but have heard about Him from others, and have put belief in Him into the back of their minds along with the various odds and ends that make up their total creed. To many others God is but an ideal, another name for goodness, or beauty, or truth; or He is law, or life, or the creative impulse back of the phenomena of existence.

These notions about God are many and varied, but they who hold them have one thing in common: they do not know God in personal experience. The possibility of intimate acquaintance with Him has not entered their minds. While admitting His existence they do not think of Him as knowable in the sense that we know things or people.

Christians, to be sure, go further than this, at least in theory. Their creed requires them to believe in the personality of God, and they have been taught to pray, "Our Father, which art in heaven." Now personality and fatherhood carry with them the idea of the possibility of personal acquaintance. This is admitted, I say, in theory, but for millions of Christians, nevertheless, God is no more real than He is to the non-Christian. They go through life trying to love an ideal and be loyal to a mere principle.

Over against all this cloudy vagueness stands the clear scriptural doctrine that God can be known in personal experience. A loving Personality dominates the Bible, walking among the trees of the garden and breathing fragrance over every scene. Always a living Person is present, speaking, pleading, loving, working, and manifesting Himself whenever and wherever His people have the receptivity necessary to receive the manifestation.

The Bible assumes as a self-evident fact that men can know God with at least the same degree of immediacy as they know any other person or thing that comes within the field of their experience. The same terms are used to express the knowledge of God as are used to express knowledge of physical things. "O taste and see that the Lord is good." "All thy garments smell of myrrh, and aloes, and cassia, out of the ivory palaces." "My sheep hear my voice." "Blessed are the pure in heart, for they shall see God." These are but four of countless such passages from the Word of God. And more important than any proof text is the fact that the whole import of the Scripture is toward this belief.

What can all this mean except that we have in our hearts organs by means of which we can know God as certainly as we know material things through our familiar five senses? We apprehend the physical world by exercising the faculties given us for the purpose, and we possess spiritual faculties by means of which we can know God and the spiritual world if we will obey the Spirit's urge and begin to use them.

That a saving work must first be done in the heart is taken for granted here. The spiritual faculties of the unregenerate man lie asleep in his nature, unused and for every purpose dead; that is the stroke which has fallen upon us by sin. They may be quickened to active life again by the operation of the Holy Spirit in regeneration; that is one of the immeasurable benefits which come to us through Christ's atoning work on the cross.

But the very ransomed children of God themselves: why do they know so little of that habitual conscious communion with God which the Scriptures seem to offer? The answer is our chronic unbelief. Faith enables our spiritual sense to function. Where faith is defective the result will be inward insensibility and numbness toward spiritual things. This is the condition of vast numbers of Christians today. No proof is necessary to support that statement. We have but to converse with the first Christian we meet or enter the first church we find open to acquire all the proof we need.

A spiritual kingdom lies all about us, enclosing us, embracing us, altogether within reach of our inner selves, waiting for us to recognize it. God Himself is here waiting our response to His Presence. This eternal world will come alive to us the moment we begin to reckon upon its reality.

I have just now used two words which demand definition; or if definition is impossible, I must at least make clear what I mean when I use them. They are "reckon" and "reality."

What do I mean by reality? I mean that which has existence apart from any idea any mind may have of it, and which would exist if there were no mind anywhere to entertain a thought of it. That which is real has being in itself. It does not depend upon the observer for its validity.

I am aware that there are those who love to poke fun at the plain man's idea of reality. They are the idealists who spin endless proofs that nothing is real outside of the mind. They are the relativists who like to show that there are no fixed points in the universe from which we can measure anything. They smile down upon us from their lofty intellectual peaks and settle us to their own satisfaction by fastening upon us the reproachful term "absolutist." The Christian is not put out of countenance by this show of contempt. He can smile right back at them, for he knows that there is only One who is Absolute, that is God. But he knows also that the Absolute One has made this world for man's uses, and, while there is nothing fixed or real in the last meaning of the words (the meaning as applied to God) for every purpose of human life we are permitted to act as if there were. And every man does act thus except the mentally sick. These unfortunates also have trouble with reality, but they are consistent; they insist upon living in accordance with their ideas of things. They are honest, and it is their very honesty that constitutes them a social problem.

The idealists and relativists are not mentally sick. They prove their soundness by living their lives according to the very notions of reality which they in theory repudiate and by counting upon the very fixed points which they prove are not there. They could earn a lot more respect for their notions if they were willing to live by them; but this they are careful not to do. Their ideas are brain-deep, not life-deep. Wherever life touches them they repudiate their theories and live like other men.

The Christian is too sincere to play with ideas for their own sake. He takes no pleasure in the mere spinning of gossamer webs for display. All his beliefs are practical. They are geared into his life. By them he lives or dies, stands or falls for this world and for all time to come. From the insincere man he turns away.

The sincere plain man knows that the world is real. He finds it here when he wakes to consciousness, and he knows that he did not think it into being. It was here waiting for him when he came, and he knows that when he prepares to leave this earthly scene it will be here still to bid him good-bye as he departs. By the deep wisdom of life he is wiser than a thousand men who doubt. He stands upon the earth and feels the wind and rain in his face and he knows that they are real. He sees the sun by day and the stars by night. He sees the hot lightning play out of the dark thundercloud. He hears the sounds of nature and the cries of human joy and pain. These he knows are real. He lies down on the cool earth at night and has no fear that it will prove illusory or fail him while he sleeps. In the morning the firm ground will be under him, the blue sky above him and the rocks and trees around him as when he closed his eyes the night before. So he lives and rejoices in a world of reality.

With his five senses he engages this real world. All things necessary to his physical existence he apprehends by the faculties with which he has been equipped by the God who created him and placed him in such a world as this.

Now, by our definition also God is real. He is real in the absolute and final sense that nothing else is. All other reality is contingent upon His. The great Reality is God who is the Author of that lower and dependent reality which makes up the sum of created things, including ourselves. God has objective existence independent of and apart from any notions which we may have concerning Him. The worshipping heart does not create its Object. It finds Him here when it wakes from its moral slumber in the morning of its regeneration.

Another word that must be cleared up is the word reckon. This does not mean to visualize or imagine. Imagination is not faith. The two are not only different from, but stand in sharp opposition to, each other. Imagination projects unreal images out of the mind and seeks to attach reality to them. Faith creates nothing; it simply reckons upon that which is already there.

God and the spiritual world are real. We can reckon upon them with as much assurance as we reckon upon the familiar world around us. Spiritual things are there (or rather we should say here') inviting our attention and challenging our trust.

Our trouble is that we have established bad thought habits. We habitually think of the visible world as real and doubt the reality of any other. We do not deny the existence of the spiritual world but we doubt that it is real in the accepted meaning of the word.

The world of sense intrudes upon our attention day and night for the whole of our lifetime. It is clamorous, insistent and self-demonstrating. It does not appeal to our faith; it is here, assaulting our five senses, demanding to be accepted as real and final. But sin has so clouded the lenses of our hearts that we cannot see that other reality, the City of God, shining around us. The world of sense triumphs. The visible becomes the enemy of the invisible; the temporal, of the eternal. That is the curse inherited by every member of Adam's tragic race.

At the root of the Christian life lies belief in the invisible. The object of the Christian's faith is unseen reality.

Our uncorrected thinking, influenced by the blindness of our natural hearts and the intrusive ubiquity of visible things, tends to draw a contrast between the spiritual and the real; but actually no such contrast exists. The antithesis lies elsewhere: between the real and the imaginary, between the spiritual and the material, between the temporal and the eternal; but between the spiritual and the real, never. The spiritual is real.

If we would rise into that region of light and power plainly beckoning us through the Scriptures of truth we must break the evil habit of ignoring the spiritual. We must shift our interest from the seen to the unseen. For the great unseen Reality is God. "He that cometh to God must believe that he is, and that he is a rewarder of them that diligently seek him." This is basic in the life of faith. From there we can rise to unlimited heights. "Ye believe in God," said our Lord Jesus Christ, "believe also in me." Without the first there can be no second.

If we truly want to follow God we must seek to be other-worldly. This I say knowing well that that word has been used with scorn by the sons of this world and applied to the Christian as a badge of reproach. So be it. Every man must choose his world. If we who follow Christ, with all the facts before us and knowing what we are about, deliberately choose the Kingdom of God as our sphere of interest I see no reason why anyone should object. If we lose by it, the loss is our own; if we gain, we rob no one by so doing. The "other world," which is the object of this world's disdain and the subject of the drunkard's mocking song, is our carefully chosen goal and the object of our holiest longing.

But we must avoid the common fault of pushing the "other world" into the future. It is not future, but present. It parallels our familiar physical world, and the doors between the two worlds are open. "Ye are come," says the writer to the Hebrews (and the tense is plainly present), "unto Mount Zion, and unto the city of the living God, the heavenly Jerusalem, and to an innumerable company of angels, to the general assembly and church of the firstborn, which are written in heaven, and to God the Judge of all, and to the spirits of just men made perfect, and to Jesus the mediator of the new covenant, and to the blood of sprinkling, that speaketh better things than that of Abel." All these things are contrasted with "the mount that might be touched" and "the sound of a trumpet and the voice of words" that might be heard. May we not safely conclude that, as the realities of Mount Sinai were apprehended by the senses, so the realities of Mount Zion are to be grasped by the soul? And this not by any trick of the imagination, but in downright actuality. The soul has eyes with which to see and ears with which to hear. Feeble they may be from long disuse, but by the life-giving touch of Christ alive now and capable of sharpest sight and most sensitive hearing.

As we begin to focus upon God the things of the spirit will take shape before our inner eyes. Obedience to the word of Christ will bring an inward revelation of the Godhead (John 14:21-23). It will give acute perception enabling us to see God even as is promised to the pure in heart. A new God-consciousness will seize upon us and we shall begin to taste and hear and inwardly feel the God who is our life and our all. There will be seen the constant shining of the light that lighteth every man that cometh into the world. More and more, as our faculties grow sharper and more sure, God will become to us the great All, and His Presence the glory and wonder of our lives.

O God, quicken to life every power within me, that I may lay hold on eternal things. Open my eyes that I may see; give me acute spiritual perception; enable me to taste Thee and know that Thou art good. Make heaven more real to me than any earthly thing has ever been. Amen.

THE UNIVERSAL PRESENCE

*Whither shall I go from thy spirit?
or whither shall I flee from thy
presence?—Psm. 139:7*

In all Christian teaching certain basic truths are found, hidden at times, and rather assumed than asserted, but necessary to all truth as the primary colors are found in and necessary to the finished painting. Such a truth is the divine immanence.

God dwells in His creation and is everywhere indivisibly present in all His works. This is boldly taught by prophet and apostle and is accepted by Christian theology generally. That is, it appears in the books, but for some reason it has not sunk into the average Christian's heart so as to become a part of his believing self. Christian teachers shy away from its full implications, and, if they mention it at all, mute it down till it has little meaning. I would guess the reason for this to be the fear of being charged with pantheism; but the doctrine of the divine Presence is definitely not pantheism.

Pantheism's error is too palpable to deceive anyone. It is that God is the sum of all created things. Nature and God are one, so that whoever touches a leaf or a stone touches God. That is of course to degrade the glory of the incorruptible Deity and, in an effort to make all things divine, banish all divinity from the world entirely.

The truth is that while God dwells in His world He is separated from it by a gulf forever impassable. However closely He may be identified with the work of His hands they are and must eternally be other than He, and He is and must be antecedent to and independent of them. He is transcendent above all His works even while He is immanent within them.

What now does the divine immanence mean in direct Christian experience? It means simply that God is here. Wherever we are, God is here. There is no place, there can be no place, where He is not. Ten million intelligences standing at as many points in space and separated by incomprehensible distances can each one say with equal truth, God is here. No point is nearer to God than any other point. It is exactly as near to God from any place as it is from any other place. No one is in mere distance any further from or any nearer to God than any other person is.

These are truths believed by every instructed Christian. It remains for us to think on them and pray over them until they begin to glow within us.

"In the beginning God." Not matter, for matter is not self-causing. It requires an antecedent cause, and God is that Cause. Not law, for law is but a name for the course which all creation follows. That course had to be planned, and the Planner is God. Not mind, for mind also is a created thing and must have a Creator back of it. In the beginning God, the uncaused Cause of matter, mind and law. There we must begin.

Adam sinned and, in his panic, frantically tried to do the impossible: he tried to hide from the Presence of God. David also must have had wild thoughts of trying to escape from the Presence, for he wrote, "Whither shall I go from thy spirit? or whither shall I flee from thy presence?" Then he proceeded through one of his most beautiful psalms to celebrate the glory of the divine immanence. "If I ascend up into heaven, thou art there: if I make my bed in hell, behold, thou art there. If I take the wings of the morning, and dwell in the uttermost parts of the sea; even there shall thy hand lead me, and thy right hand shall hold me." And he knew that God's being and God's seeing are the same, that the seeing Presence had been with him even before he was born, watching the mystery of unfolding life. Solomon exclaimed, "But will God indeed dwell on the earth? behold the heaven and the heaven of heavens cannot contain thee: how much less this house which I have builded." Paul assured the Athenians that "God is not far from any one of us: for in him we live, and move, and have our being."

If God is present at every point in space, if we cannot go where He is not, cannot even conceive of a place where He is not, why then has not that Presence become the one universally celebrated fact of the world? The patriarch Jacob, "in the waste howling wilderness," gave the answer to that question. He saw a vision of God and cried out in wonder, "Surely the Lord is in this place; and I knew it not." Jacob had never been for one small division of a moment outside the circle of that all-pervading Presence. But he knew it not. That was his trouble, and it is ours. Men do not know that God is here. What a difference it would make if they knew.

The Presence and the manifestation of the Presence are not the same. There can be the one without the other. God is here when we are wholly unaware of it. He is manifest only when and as we are aware of His Presence. On our part there must be surrender to the Spirit of God, for His work it is to show us the Father and the Son. If we co-operate with Him in loving obedience God will manifest Himself to us, and that manifestation will be the difference between a nominal Christian life and a life radiant with the light of His face.

Always, everywhere God is present, and always He seeks to discover Himself. To each one he would reveal not only that He is, but what He is as well. He did not have to be persuaded to discover Himself to Moses. "And the Lord descended in the cloud, and stood with him there, and proclaimed the name of the Lord." He not only made a verbal proclamation of His nature but He revealed His very Self to Moses so that the skin of Moses' face shone with the supernatural light. It will be a great moment for some of us when we begin to believe that God's promise of self-revelation is literally true: that He promised much, but promised no more than He intends to fulfill.

Our pursuit of God is successful just because He is forever seeking to manifest Himself to us. The revelation of God to any man is not God coming from a distance upon a time to pay a brief and momentous visit to the man's soul. Thus to think of it is to misunderstand it all. The approach of God to the soul or of the soul to God is not to be thought of in spatial terms at all. There is no idea of physical distance involved in the concept. It is not a matter of miles but of experience.

To speak of being near to or far from God is to use language in a sense always understood when applied to our ordinary human relationships. A man may say, 'I feel that my son is coming nearer to me as he gets older," and yet that son has lived by his father's side since he was born and has never been away from home more than a day or so in his entire life. What then can the father mean? Obviously, he is speaking of experience. He means that the boy is coming to know him more intimately and with deeper understanding, that the barriers of thought and feeling between the two are disappearing, that father and son are becoming more closely united in mind and heart.

So when we sing, "Draw me nearer, nearer, blessed Lord," we are not thinking of the nearness of place, but of the nearness of relationship. It is for increasing degrees of awareness that we pray, for a more perfect consciousness of the divine Presence. We need never shout across the spaces to an absent God. He is nearer than our own soul, closer than our most secret thoughts.

Why do some persons "find" God in a way that others do not? Why does God manifest His Presence to some and let multitudes of others struggle along in the half-light of imperfect Christian experience? Of course the will of God is the same for all. He has no favorites within His household. All He has ever done for any of His children He will do for all of His children. The difference lies not with God but with us.

Pick at random a score of great saints whose lives and testimonies are widely known. Let them be Bible characters or well known Christians of post-Biblical times. You will be struck instantly with the fact that the saints were not alike. Sometimes the unlikenesses were so great as to be positively glaring. How different for example was Moses from Isaiah; how different was Elijah from David; how unlike each other were John and Paul, St. Francis and Luther, Finney and Thomas à Kempis. The differences are as wide as human life itself: differences of race, nationality, education, temperament, habit and personal qualities. Yet they all walked, each in his day, upon a high road of spiritual living far above the common way.

Their differences must have been incidental and in the eyes of God of no significance. In some vital quality they must have been alike. What was it?

I venture to suggest that the one vital quality which they had in common was spiritual receptivity. Something in them was open to heaven, something which urged them Godward. Without attempting anything like a profound analysis I shall say simply that they had spiritual awareness and that they went on to cultivate it until it became the biggest thing in their lives. They differed from the average person in that when they felt the inward longing they did something about it. They acquired the lifelong habit of spiritual response. They were not disobedient to the heavenly vision. As David put it neatly, "When thou saidst, Seek ye my face; my heart said unto thee, Thy face, Lord, will I seek."

As with everything good in human life, back of this receptivity is God. The sovereignty of God is here, and is felt even by those who have not placed particular stress upon it theologically. The pious Michael Angelo confessed this in a sonnet:

> *My unassisted heart is barren clay,*
> *That of its native self can nothing feed:*
> *Of good and pious works Thou art the seed,*
> *That quickens only where Thou sayest it may:*
> *Unless Thou show to us Thine own true way*
> *No man can find it: Father! Thou must lead.*

These words will repay study as the deep and serious testimony of a great Christian.

Important as it is that we recognize God working in us, I would yet warn against a too-great preoccupation with the thought. It is a sure road to sterile passivity. God will not hold us responsible to understand the mysteries of election, predestination and the divine sovereignty. The best and safest way to deal with these truths is to raise our eyes to God and in deepest reverence say, "O Lord, Thou knowest." Those things belong to the deep and mysterious Profound of God's omniscience. Prying into them may make theologians, but it will never make saints.

Receptivity is not a single thing; it is a compound rather, a blending of several elements within the soul. It is an affinity for, a bent toward, a sympathetic response to, a desire to have. From this it may be gathered that it can be present in degrees, that we may have little or more or less, depending upon the individual. It may be increased by exercise or destroyed by neglect. It is not a sovereign and irresistible force which comes upon us as a seizure from above. It is a gift of God, indeed, but one which must be recognized and cultivated as any other gift if it is to realize the purpose for which it was given.

Failure to see this is the cause of a very serious breakdown in modern evangelicalism. The idea of cultivation and exercise, so dear to the saints of old, has now no place in our total religious picture. It is too slow, too common. We now demand glamour and fast flowing dramatic action. A generation of Christians reared among push buttons and automatic machines is impatient of slower and less direct methods of reaching their goals. We have been trying to apply machine age methods to our relations with God. We read our chapter, have our short devotions and rush away, hoping to make up for our deep inward bankruptcy by attending another gospel meeting or listening to another thrilling story told by a religious adventurer lately returned from afar.

The tragic results of this spirit are all about us. Shallow lives, hollow religious philosophies, the preponderance of the element of fun in gospel meetings, the glorification of men, trust in religious externalities, quasi-religious fellowships, salesmanship methods, the mistaking of dynamic personality for the power of the Spirit: these and such as these are the symptoms of an evil disease, a deep and serious malady of the soul.

For this great sickness that is upon us no one person is responsible, and no Christian is wholly free from blame. We have all contributed, directly or indirectly, to this sad state of affairs. We have been too blind to see, or too timid to speak out, or too self-satisfied to desire anything better than the poor average diet with which others appear satisfied. To put it differently, we have accepted one another's notions, copied one another's lives and made one another's experiences the model for our own. And for a generation the trend has been downward. Now we have reached a low place of sand and burnt wire grass and, worst of all, we have made the Word of Truth conform to our experience and accepted this low plane as the very pasture of the blessed.

It will require a determined heart and more than a little courage to wrench ourselves loose from the grip of our times and return to Biblical ways. But it can be done. Every now and then in the past Christians have had to do it. History has recorded several large-scale returns led by such men as St. Francis, Martin Luther and George Fox. Unfortunately there seems to be no Luther or Fox on the horizon at present. Whether or not another such return may be expected before the coming of Christ is a question upon which Christians are not fully agreed, but that is not of too great importance to us now.

What God in His sovereignty may yet do on a world-scale I do not claim to know: but what He will do for the plain man or woman who seeks His face I believe I do know and can tell others. Let any man turn to God in earnest, let him begin to exercise himself unto godliness, let him seek to develop his powers of spiritual receptivity by trust and obedience and humility, and the results will exceed anything he may have hoped in his leaner and weaker days.

Any man who by repentance and a sincere return to God will break himself out of the mold in which he has been held, and will go to the Bible itself for his spiritual standards, will be delighted with what he finds there.

Let us say it again: The Universal Presence is a fact. God is here. The whole universe is alive with His life. And He is no strange or foreign God, but the familiar Father of our Lord Jesus Christ whose love has for these thousands of years enfolded the sinful race of men. And always He is trying to get our attention, to reveal Himself to us, to communicate with us. We have within us the ability to know Him if we will but respond to His overtures. (And this we call pursuing God!) We will know Him in increasing degree as our receptivity becomes more perfect by faith and love and practice.

O God and Father, I repent of my sinful preoccupation with visible things. The world has been too much with me. Thou hast been here and I knew it not. I have been blind to Thy Presence. Open my eyes that I may behold Thee in and around me. For Christ's sake, Amen.

The Speaking Voice

*In the beginning was the Word,
and the Word was with God, and
the Word was God.—John 1:1*

An intelligent plain man, untaught in the truths of Christianity, coming upon this text, would likely conclude that John meant to teach that it is the nature of God to speak, to communicate His thoughts to others. And he would be right. A word is a medium by which thoughts are expressed, and the application of the term to the Eternal Son leads us to believe that self-expression is inherent in the Godhead, that God is forever seeking to speak Himself out to His creation. The whole Bible supports the idea. God is speaking. Not God spoke, but God is speaking. He is by His nature continuously articulate. He fills the world with His speaking Voice.

One of the great realities with which we have to deal is the Voice of God in His world. The briefest and only satisfying cosmogony is this: "He spake and it was done." The why of natural law is the living Voice of God immanent in His creation. And this word of God which brought all worlds into being cannot be understood to mean the Bible, for it is not a written or printed word at all, but the expression of the will of God spoken into the structure of all things. This word of God is the breath of God filling the world with living potentiality. The Voice of God is the most powerful force in nature, indeed the only force in nature, for all energy is here only because the power-filled Word is being spoken.

The Bible is the written word of God, and because it is written it is confined and limited by the necessities of ink and paper and leather. The Voice of God, however, is alive and free as the sovereign God is free. "The words that I speak unto you, they are spirit, and they are life." The life is in the speaking words. God's word in the Bible can have power only because it corresponds to God's word in the universe. It is the present Voice which makes the written Word all-powerful. Otherwise it would lie locked in slumber within the covers of a book.

We take a low and primitive view of things when we conceive of God at the creation coming into physical contact with things, shaping and fitting and building like a carpenter. The Bible teaches otherwise: "By the word of the Lord were the heavens made; and all the host of them by the breath of his mouth. . . . For he spake, and it was done; he commanded, and it stood fast." "Through faith we understand that the worlds were framed by the word of God." Again we must remember that God is referring here not to His written Word, but to His speaking Voice. His world-filling Voice is meant, that Voice which antedates the Bible by uncounted centuries, that Voice which has not been silent since the dawn of creation, but is sounding still throughout the full far reaches of the universe.

The Word of God is quick and powerful. In the beginning He spoke to nothing, and it became something. Chaos heard it and became order, darkness heard it and became light. "And God said—and it was so." These twin phrases, as cause and effect, occur throughout the Genesis story of the creation. The said accounts for the so. The so is the said put into the continuous present.

That God is here and that He is speaking—these truths are back of all other Bible truths; without them there could be no revelation at all. God did not write a book and send it by messenger to be read at a distance by unaided minds. He spoke a Book and lives in His spoken words, constantly speaking His words and causing the power of them to persist across the years. God breathed on clay and it became a man; He breathes on men and they become clay. "Return ye children of men," was the word spoken at the Fall by which God decreed the death of every man, and no added word has He needed to speak. The sad procession of mankind across the face of the earth from birth to the grave is proof that His original Word was enough.

We have not given sufficient attention to that deep utterance in the Book of John, 'That was the true Light, which lighteth every man that cometh into the world." Shift the punctuation around as we will and the truth is still there: the Word of God affects the hearts of all men as light in the soul. In the hearts of all men the light shines, the Word sounds, and there is no escaping them. Something like this would of necessity be so if God is alive and in His world. And John says that it is so. Even those persons who have never heard of the Bible have still been preached to with sufficient clarity to remove every excuse from their hearts forever. "Which show the work of the law written in their hearts, their conscience also bearing witness, and their thoughts the mean while either accusing or else excusing one another." "For the invisible things of him from the creation of the world are clearly seen, being understood by the things that are made, even his eternal power and Godhead; so that they are without excuse."

This universal Voice of God was by the ancient Hebrews often called Wisdom, and was said to be everywhere sounding and searching throughout the earth, seeking some response from the sons of men. The eighth chapter of the Book of Proverbs begins, "Doth not wisdom cry? and understanding put forth her voice?" The writer then pictures wisdom as a beautiful woman standing "in the top of the high places, by the way in the places of the paths." She sounds her voice from every quarter so that no one may miss hearing it. "Unto you, O men, I call; and my voice is to the sons of men." Then she pleads for the simple and the foolish to give ear to her words. It is spiritual response for which this Wisdom of God is pleading, a response which she has always sought and is but rarely able to secure. The tragedy is that our eternal welfare depends upon our hearing, and we have trained our ears not to hear.

This universal Voice has ever sounded, and it has often troubled men even when they did not understand the source of their fears. Could it be that this Voice distilling like a living mist upon the hearts of men has been the undiscovered cause of the troubled conscience and the longing for immortality confessed by millions since the dawn of recorded history? We need not fear to face up to this. The speaking Voice is a fact. How men have reacted to it is for any observer to note.

When God spoke out of heaven to our Lord, self-centered men who heard it explained it by natural causes: they said, "It thundered." This habit of explaining the Voice by appeals to natural law is at the very root of modern science. In the living breathing cosmos there is a mysterious Something, too wonderful, too awful for any mind to understand. The believing man does not claim to understand. He falls to his knees and whispers, "God." The man of earth kneels also, but not to worship. He kneels to examine, to search, to find the cause and the how of things. Just now we happen to be living in a secular age. Our thought habits are those of the scientist, not those of the worshipper. We are more likely to explain than to adore. "It thundered," we exclaim, and go our earthly way. But still the Voice sounds and searches. The order and life of the world depend upon that Voice, but men are mostly too busy or too stubborn to give attention.

Everyone of us has had experiences which we have not been able to explain: a sudden sense of loneliness, or a feeling of wonder or awe in the face of the universal vastness. Or we have had a fleeting visitation of light like an illumination from some other sun, giving us in a quick flash an assurance that we are from another world, that our origins are divine. What we saw there, or felt, or heard, may have been contrary to all that we had been taught in the schools and at wide variance with all our former beliefs and opinions. We were forced to suspend our acquired doubts while, for a moment, the clouds were rolled back and we saw and heard for ourselves. Explain such things as we will, I think we have not been fair to the facts until we allow at least the possibility that such experiences may arise from the Presence of God in the world and His persistent effort to communicate with mankind. Let us not dismiss such an hypothesis too flippantly.

It is my own belief (and here I shall not feel bad if no one follows me) that every good and beautiful thing which man has produced in the world has been the result of his faulty and sin-blocked response to the creative Voice sounding over the earth. The moral philosophers who dreamed their high dreams of virtue, the religious thinkers who speculated about God and immortality, the poets and artists who created out of common stuff pure and lasting beauty: how can we explain them? It is not enough to say simply, "It was genius." What then is genius? Could it be that a genius is a man haunted by the speaking Voice, laboring and striving like one possessed to achieve ends which he only vaguely understands? That the great man may have missed God in his labors, that he may even have spoken or written against God does not destroy the idea I am advancing. God's redemptive revelation in the Holy Scriptures is necessary to saving faith and peace with God. Faith in a risen Saviour is necessary if the vague stirrings toward immortality are to bring us to restful and satisfying communion with God. To me this is a plausible explanation of all that is best out of Christ. But you can be a good Christian and not accept my thesis.

The Voice of God is a friendly Voice. No one need fear to listen to it unless he has already made up his mind to resist it. The blood of Jesus has covered not only the human race but all creation as well. "And having made peace through the blood of his cross, by him to reconcile all things unto himself; by him, I say, whether they be things in earth, or things in heaven." We may safely preach a friendly Heaven. The heavens as well as the earth are filled with the good will of Him that dwelt in the bush. The perfect blood of atonement secures this forever.

Whoever will listen will hear the speaking Heaven. This is definitely not the hour when men take kindly to an exhortation to listen, for listening is not today a part of popular religion. We are at the opposite end of the pole from there. Religion has accepted the monstrous heresy that noise, size, activity and bluster make a man dear to God. But we may take heart. To a people caught in the tempest of the last great conflict

God says, "Be still, and know that I am God," and still He says it, as if He means to tell us that our strength and safety lie not in noise but in silence.

It is important that we get still to wait on God. And it is best that we get alone, preferably with our Bible outspread before us. Then if we will we may draw near to God and begin to hear Him speak to us in our hearts. I think for the average person the progression will be something like this: First a sound as of a Presence walking in the garden. Then a voice, more intelligible, but still far from clear. Then the happy moment when the Spirit begins to illuminate the Scriptures, and that which had been only a sound, or at best a voice, now becomes an intelligible word, warm and intimate and clear as the word of a dear friend. Then will come life and light, and best of all, ability to see and rest in and embrace Jesus Christ as Saviour and Lord and All.

The Bible will never be a living Book to us until we are convinced that God is articulate in His universe. To jump from a dead, impersonal world to a dogmatic Bible is too much for most people. They may admit that they should accept the Bible as the Word of God, and they may try to think of it as such, but they find it impossible to believe that the words there on the page are actually for them. A man may say, "These words are addressed to me," and yet in his heart not feel and know that they are. He is the victim of a divided psychology. He tries to think of God as mute everywhere else and vocal only in a book.

I believe that much of our religious unbelief is due to a wrong conception of and a wrong feeling for the Scriptures of Truth. A silent God suddenly began to speak in a book and when the book was finished lapsed back into silence again forever. Now we read the book as the record of what God said when He was for a brief time in a speaking mood. With notions like that in our heads how can we believe? The facts are that God is not silent, has never been silent. It is the nature of God to speak. The second Person of the Holy Trinity is called the Word. The Bible is the inevitable outcome of God's continuous speech. It is the infallible declaration of His mind for us put into our familiar human words.

I think a new world will arise out of the religious mists when we approach our Bible with the idea that it is not only a book which was once spoken, but a book which is now speaking. The prophets habitually said, "Thus saith the Lord." They meant their hearers to understand that God's speaking is in the continuous present. We may use the past tense properly to indicate that at a certain time a certain word of God was spoken, but a word of God once spoken continues to be spoken, as a child once born continues to be alive, or a world once created continues to exist. And those are but imperfect illustrations, for children die and worlds burn out, but the Word of our God endureth forever.

If you would follow on to know the Lord, come at once to the open Bible expecting it to speak to you. Do not come with the notion that it is a thing which you may push around at your convenience. It is more than a thing, it is a voice, a word, the very Word of the living God.

Lord, teach me to listen. The times are noisy and my ears are weary with the thousand raucous sounds which continuously assault them. Give me the spirit of the boy Samuel when he said to Thee, "Speak, for thy servant heareth." Let me hear Thee speaking in my heart. Let me get used to the sound of Thy Voice, that its tones may be familiar when the sounds of earth die away and the only sound will be the music of Thy speaking Voice. Amen.

THE GAZE OF THE SOUL

*Looking unto Jesus the author and
finisher of our faith.— Heb. 12:2*

Let us think of our intelligent plain man mentioned in chapter six coming for the first time to the reading of the Scriptures. He approaches the Bible without any previous knowledge of what it contains. He is wholly without prejudice; he has nothing to prove and nothing to defend.

Such a man will not have read long until his mind begins to observe certain truths standing out from the page. They are the spiritual principles behind the record of God's dealings with men, and woven into the writings of holy men as they "were moved by the Holy Ghost." As he reads on he might want to number these truths as they become clear to him and make a brief summary under each number. These summaries will be the tenets of his Biblical creed. Further reading will not affect these points except to enlarge and strengthen them. Our man is finding out what the Bible actually teaches.

High up on the list of things which the Bible teaches will be the doctrine of faith. The place of weighty importance which the Bible gives to faith will be too plain for him to miss. He will very likely conclude: Faith is all-important in the life of the soul. Without faith it is impossible to please God. Faith will get me anything, take me anywhere in the Kingdom of God, but without faith there can be no approach to God, no forgiveness, no deliverance, no salvation, no communion, no spiritual life at all.

By the time our friend has reached the eleventh chapter of Hebrews the eloquent encomium which is there pronounced upon faith will not seem strange to him. He will have read Paul's powerful defense of faith in his Roman and Galatian epistles. Later if he goes on to study church history he will understand the amazing power in the teachings of the Reformers as they showed the central place of faith in the Christian religion.

Now if faith is so vitally important, if it is an indispensable must in our pursuit of God, it is perfectly natural that we should be deeply concerned over whether or not we possess this most precious gift. And our minds being what they are, it is inevitable that sooner or later we should get around to inquiring after the nature of faith. What is faith? would lie close to the question, Do I have faith? and would demand an answer if it were anywhere to be found.

Almost all who preach or write on the subject of faith have much the same things to say concerning it. They tell us that it is believing a promise, that it is taking God at His word, that it is reckoning the Bible to be true and stepping out upon it. The rest of the book or sermon is usually taken up with stories of persons who have had their prayers answered as a result of their faith. These answers are mostly direct gifts of a practical and temporal nature such as health, money, physical protection or success in business. Or if the teacher is of a philosophic turn of mind he may take another course and lose us in a welter of metaphysics or snow us under with psychological jargon as he defines and re-defines, paring the slender hair of faith thinner and thinner till it disappears in gossamer shavings at last. When he is finished we get up disappointed and go out "by that same door where in we went." Surely there must be something better than this.

In the Scriptures there is practically no effort made to define faith. Outside of a brief fourteen-word definition in Hebrews 11:1, I know of no Biblical definition, and even there faith is defined functionally, not philosophically; that is, it is a statement of what faith is in operation, not what it is in essence. It assumes the presence of faith and shows what it results in, rather than what it is. We will be wise to go just that far and attempt to go no further. We are told from whence it comes and by what means: "Faith is a gift of God," and "Faith cometh by hearing, and hearing by the word of God." This much is clear, and, to paraphrase Thomas à Kempis, "I had rather exercise faith than know the definition thereof."

From here on, when the words "faith is" or their equivalent occur in this chapter I ask that they be understood to refer to what faith is in operation as exercised by a believing man. Right here we drop the notion of definition and think about faith as it may be experienced in action. The complexion of our thoughts will be practical, not theoretical.

In a dramatic story in the Book of Numbers faith is seen in action. Israel became discouraged and spoke against God, and the Lord sent fiery serpents among them. "And they bit the people; and much people of Israel died." Then Moses sought the Lord for them and He heard and gave them a remedy against the bite of the serpents. He commanded

Moses to make a serpent of brass and put it upon a pole in sight of all the people, "and it shall come to pass, that everyone that is bitten, when he looketh upon it, shall live." Moses obeyed, "and it came to pass, that if a serpent had bitten any man, when he beheld the serpent of brass, he lived" (Num. 21:4-9).

In the New Testament this important bit of history is interpreted for us by no less an authority than our Lord Jesus Christ Himself. He is explaining to His hearers how they may be saved. He tells them that it is by believing. Then to make it clear He refers to this incident in the Book of Numbers. "As Moses lifted up the serpent in the wilderness, even so must the Son of man be lifted up: that whosoever believeth in him should not perish, but have eternal life" (John 3:14-15).

Our plain man in reading this would make an important discovery. He would notice that "look" and "believe" were synonymous terms. "Looking" on the Old Testament serpent is identical with "believing" on the New Testament Christ. That is, the looking and the believing are the same thing. And he would understand that while Israel looked with their external eyes, believing is done with the heart. I think he would conclude that faith is the gaze of a soul upon a saving God.

When he had seen this he would remember passages he had read before, and their meaning would come flooding over him. "They looked unto him, and were lightened: and their faces were not ashamed" (Psa. 34:5). "Unto thee lift I up mine eyes, O thou that dwellest in the heavens. Behold, as the eyes of servants look unto the hand of their masters, and as the eyes of a maiden unto the hand of her mistress; so our eyes wait upon the Lord our God, until that he have mercy upon us" (Psa. 123:1-2). Here the man seeking mercy looks straight at the God of mercy and never takes his eyes away from Him till mercy is granted. And our Lord Himself looked always at God. "Looking up to heaven, he blessed, and brake, and gave the bread to his disciples" (Matt. 14:19). Indeed Jesus taught that He wrought His works by always keeping His inward eyes upon His Father. His power lay in His continuous look at God (John 5:19-21).

In full accord with the few texts we have quoted is the whole tenor of the inspired Word. It is summed up for us in the Hebrew epistle when we are instructed to run life's race "looking unto Jesus the author and finisher of our faith." From all this we learn that faith is not a once-done act, but a continuous gaze of the heart at the Triune God.

Believing, then, is directing the heart's attention to Jesus. It is lifting the mind to "behold the Lamb of God," and never ceasing that beholding for the rest of our lives. At first this may be difficult, but it becomes easier as we look steadily at His wondrous Person, quietly and without strain. Distractions may hinder, but once the heart is committed to Him, after each brief excursion away from Him the attention will return again and rest upon Him like a wandering bird coming back to its window.

I would emphasize this one committal, this one great volitional act which establishes the heart's intention to gaze forever upon Jesus. God takes this intention for our choice and makes what allowances He must for the thousand distractions which beset us in this evil world. He knows that we have set the direction of our hearts toward Jesus, and we can know it too, and comfort ourselves with the knowledge that a habit of soul is forming which will become after a while a sort of spiritual reflex requiring no more conscious effort on our part.

Faith is the least self-regarding of the virtues. It is by its very nature scarcely conscious of its own existence. Like the eye which sees everything in front of it and never sees itself, faith is occupied with the Object upon which it rests and pays no attention to itself at all. While we are looking at God we do not see ourselves—blessed riddance. The man who has struggled to purify himself and has had nothing but repeated failures will experience real relief when he stops tinkering with his soul and looks away to the perfect One. While he looks at Christ the very things he has so long been trying to do will be getting done within him. It will be God working in him to will and to do.

Faith is not in itself a meritorious act; the merit is in the One toward Whom it is directed. Faith is a redirecting of our sight, a getting out of the focus of our own vision and getting God into focus. Sin has twisted our vision inward and made it self-regarding. Unbelief has put self where God should be, and is perilously close to the sin of Lucifer who said, "I will set my throne above the throne of God." Faith looks out instead of in and the whole life falls into line.

All this may seem too simple. But we have no apology to make. To those who would seek to climb into heaven after help or descend into hell God says, "The word is nigh thee, even the word of faith." The word induces us to lift up our eyes unto the Lord and the blessed work of faith begins.

When we lift our inward eyes to gaze upon God we are sure to meet friendly eyes gazing back at us, for it is written that the eyes of the Lord run to and for throughout all the earth. The sweet language of experience is "Thou God seest me." When the eyes of the soul looking out meet the eyes of God looking in, heaven has begun right here on this earth.

"When all my endeavour is turned toward Thee because all Thy endeavour is turned toward me; when I look unto Thee alone with all my attention, nor ever turn aside the eyes of my mind, because Thou dost enfold me with Thy constant regard; when I direct my love toward Thee alone because Thou, who art Love's self hast turned Thee toward me alone. And what, Lord, is my life, save that embrace wherein Thy delightsome sweetness doth so lovingly enfold me?"[1] So wrote Nicholas of Cusa four hundred years ago.

I should like to say more about this old man of God. He is not much known today anywhere among Christian believers, and among current Fundamentalists he is known not at all. I feel that we could gain much from a little acquaintance with men of his spiritual flavor and the school of Christian thought which they represent. Christian literature, to be accepted and approved by the evangelical leaders of our times, must follow very closely the same train of thought, a kind of "party line" from which it is scarcely safe to depart. A half-century of this in America has made us smug and content. We imitate each other with slavish devotion and our most strenuous efforts are put forth to try to say the same thing that everyone around us is saying —and yet to find an excuse for saying it, some little safe variation on the approved theme or, if no more, at least a new illustration.

Nicholas was a true follower of Christ, a lover of the Lord, radiant and shining in his devotion to the Person of Jesus. His theology was orthodox, but fragrant and sweet as everything about Jesus might properly be expected to be. His conception of eternal life, for instance, is beautiful in itself and, if I mistake not, is nearer in spirit to John 17:3 than that which is current among us today. Life eternal, says Nicholas, is "nought other than that blessed regard wherewith Thou never ceasest to behold me, yea, even the secret places of my soul. With Thee, to behold is to give life; 'tis unceasingly to impart sweetest love of Thee; 'tis to inflame me to love of Thee by love's imparting, and to feed me by inflaming, and by feeding to kindle my yearning, and by kindling to make me drink of the dew of gladness, and by drinking to infuse in me a fountain of life, and by infusing to make it increase and endure."[2]

Now, if faith is the gaze of the heart at God, and if this gaze is but the raising of the inward eyes to meet the all-seeing eyes of God, then it follows that it is one of the easiest things possible to do. It would be like God to make the most vital thing easy and place it within the range of possibility for the weakest and poorest of us.

---

[1] Nicholas of Cusa, The Vision of God, E. P. Dutton & Co., Inc., New York, 1928. This and the following quotations used by kind permission of the publishers.
[2] The Vision of God.

Several conclusions may fairly be drawn from all this. The simplicity of it, for instance. Since believing is looking, it can be done without special equipment or religious paraphernalia. God has seen to it that the one life-and-death essential can never be subject to the caprice of accident. Equipment can break down or get lost, water can leak away, records can be destroyed by fire, the minister can be delayed or the church burn down. All these are external to the soul and are subject to accident or mechanical failure: but looking is of the heart and can be done successfully by any man standing up or kneeling down or lying in his last agony a thousand miles from any church.

Since believing is looking it can be done any time. No season is superior to another season for this sweetest of all acts. God never made salvation depend upon new moons nor holy days or sabbaths. A man is not nearer to Christ on Easter Sunday than he is, say, on Saturday, August 3, or Monday, October 4. As long as Christ sits on the mediatorial throne every day is a good day and all days are days of salvation.

Neither does place matter in this blessed work of believing God. Lift your heart and let it rest upon Jesus and you are instantly in a sanctuary though it be a Pullman berth or a factory or a kitchen. You can see God from anywhere if your mind is set to love and obey Him.

Now, someone may ask, "Is not this of which you speak for special persons such as monks or ministers who have by the nature of their calling more time to devote to quiet meditation? I am a busy worker and have little time to spend alone." I am happy to say that the life I describe is for everyone of God's children regardless of calling. It is, in fact, happily practiced every day by many hard working persons and is beyond the reach of none.

Many have found the secret of which I speak and, without giving much thought to what is going on within them, constantly practice this habit of inwardly gazing upon God. They know that something inside their hearts sees God. Even when they are compelled to withdraw their conscious attention in order to engage in earthly affairs there is within them a secret communion always going on. Let their attention but be released for a moment from necessary business and it flies at once to God again. This has been the testimony of many Christians, so many that even as I state it thus I have a feeling that I am quoting, though from whom or from how many I cannot possibly know.

I do not want to leave the impression that the ordinary means of grace have no value. They most assuredly have. Private prayer should be practiced by every Christian. Long periods of Bible meditation will purify our gaze and direct it; church attendance will enlarge our outlook and increase our love for others. Service and work and activity; all are good and should be engaged in by every Christian. But at the bottom of all these things, giving meaning to them, will be the inward habit of beholding God. A new set of eyes (so to speak) will develop within us enabling us to be looking at God while our outward eyes are seeing the scenes of this passing world.

Someone may fear that we are magnifying private religion out of all proportion, that the "us" of the New Testament is being displaced by a selfish "I." Has it ever occurred to you that one hundred pianos all tuned to the same fork are automatically tuned to each other? They are of one accord by being tuned, not to each other, but to another standard to which each one must individually bow. So one hundred worshippers met together, each one looking away to Christ, are in heart nearer to each other than they could possibly be were they to become "unity" conscious and turn their eyes away from God to strive for closer fellowship. Social religion is perfected when private religion is purified. The body becomes stronger as its members become healthier. The whole Church of God gains when the members that compose it begin to seek a better and a higher life.

All the foregoing presupposes true repentance and a full committal of the life to God. It is hardly necessary to mention this, for only persons who have made such a committal will have read this far.

When the habit of inwardly gazing Godward becomes fixed within us we shall be ushered onto a new level of spiritual life more in keeping with the promises of God and the mood of the New Testament. The Triune God will be our dwelling place even while our feet walk the low road of simple duty here among men. We will have found life's summum bonum indeed. "There is the source of all delights that can be desired; not only can nought better be thought out by men and angels, but nought better can exist in any mode of being! For it is the absolute maximum of every rational desire, than which a greater cannot be."[3]

O Lord, I have heard a good word inviting me to look away to Thee and be satisfied. My heart longs to respond, but sin has clouded my vision till I see Thee but dimly. Be pleased to cleanse me in Thine own precious blood, and make me inwardly pure, so that I may with unveiled eyes gaze upon Thee all the days of my earthly pilgrimage. Then shall I be prepared to behold Thee in full splendor in the day when Thou shalt appear to be glorified in Thy saints and admired in all them that believe. Amen.

---

3   The Vision of God

RESTORING THE CREATOR-CREATURE RELATION

*Be thou exalted, O God, above the heavens;
let thy glory be above all the earth. —Psa. 57:5*

It is a truism to say that order in nature depends upon right relationships; to achieve harmony each thing must be in its proper position relative to each other thing. In human life it is not otherwise.

I have hinted before in these chapters that the cause of all our human miseries is a radical moral dislocation, an upset in our relation to God and to each other. For whatever else the Fall may have been, it was most certainly a sharp change in man's relation to his Creator. He adopted toward God an altered attitude, and by so doing destroyed the proper Creator-creature relation in which, unknown to him, his true happiness lay. Essentially salvation is the restoration of a right relation between man and his Creator, a bringing back to normal of the Creator-creature relation.

A satisfactory spiritual life will begin with a complete change in relation between God and the sinner; not a judicial change merely, but a conscious and experienced change affecting the sinner's whole nature. The atonement in Jesus' blood makes such a change judicially possible and the working of the Holy Spirit makes it emotionally satisfying. The story of the prodigal son perfectly illustrates this latter phase. He had brought a world of trouble upon himself by forsaking the position which he had properly held as son of his father. At bottom his restoration was nothing more than a re-establishing of the father-son relation which had existed from his birth and had been altered temporarily by his act of sinful rebellion. This story overlooks the legal aspects of redemption, but it makes beautifully clear the experiential aspects of salvation.

In determining relationships we must begin somewhere. There must be somewhere a fixed center against which everything else is measured, where the law of relativity does not enter and we can say "IS" and make no allowances. Such a center is God. When God would make His Name known to mankind He could find no better word than "I AM." When He speaks in the first person He says, "I AM"; when we speak of Him we say, "He is"; when we speak to Him we say, "Thou art." Everyone and everything else measures from that fixed point. "I am that I am," says God, "I change not."

As the sailor locates his position on the sea by "shooting" the sun, so we may get our moral bearings by looking at God. We must begin with God. We are right when and only when we stand in a right position relative to God, and we are wrong so far and so long as we stand in any other position.

Much of our difficulty as seeking Christians stems from our unwillingness to take God as He is and adjust our lives accordingly. We insist upon trying to modify Him and to bring Him nearer to our own image. The flesh whimpers against the rigor of God's inexorable sentence and begs like Agag for a little mercy, a little indulgence of its carnal ways. It is no use. We can get a right start only by accepting God as He is and learning to love Him for what He is. As we go on to know Him better we shall find it a source of unspeakable joy that God is just what He is. Some of the most rapturous moments we know will be those we spend in reverent admiration of the Godhead. In those holy moments the very thought of change in Him will be too painful to endure.

So let us begin with God. Back of all, above all, before all is God; first in sequential order, above in rank and station, exalted in dignity and honor. As the self-existent One He gave being to all things, and all things exist out of Him and for Him. "Thou art worthy, O Lord, to receive glory and honour and power: for thou hast created all things, and for thy pleasure they are and were created."

Every soul belongs to God and exists by His pleasure. God being Who and What He is, and we being who and what we are, the only thinkable relation between us is one of full lordship on His part and complete submission on ours. We owe Him every honor that it is in our power to give Him. Our everlasting grief lies in giving Him anything less.

The pursuit of God will embrace the labor of bringing our total personality into conformity to His. And this not judicially, but actually. I do not here refer to the act of justification by faith in Christ. I speak of a voluntary exalting of God to His proper station over us and a willing surrender of our whole being to the place of worshipful submission which the Creator-creature circumstance makes proper.

The moment we make up our minds that we are going on with this determination to exalt God over all we step out of the world's parade. We shall find ourselves out of adjustment to the ways of the world, and increasingly so as we make progress in the holy way. We shall acquire a new viewpoint; a new and different psychology will be formed within us; a new power will begin to surprise us by its upsurgings and its outgoings.

Our break with the world will be the direct outcome of our changed relation to God. For the world of fallen men does not honor God. Millions call themselves by His Name, it is true, and pay some token respect to Him, but a simple test will show how little He is really honored among them. Let the average man be put to the proof on the question of who is above, and his true position will be exposed. Let him be forced into making a choice between God and money, between God and men, between God and personal ambition, God and self, God and human love, and God will take second place every time. Those other things will be exalted above. However the man may protest, the proof is in the choices he makes day after day throughout his life.

"Be thou exalted" is the language of victorious spiritual experience. It is a little key to unlock the door to great treasures of grace. It is central in the life of God in the soul. Let the seeking man reach a place where life and lips join to say continually "Be thou exalted," and a thousand minor problems will be solved at once. His Christian life ceases to be the complicated thing it had been before and becomes the very essence of simplicity. By the exercise of his will he has set his course, and on that course he will stay as if guided by an automatic pilot. If blown off course for a moment by some adverse wind he will surely return again as by a secret bent of the soul. The hidden motions of the Spirit are working in his favor, and "the stars in their courses" fight for him. He has met his life problem at its center, and everything else must follow along.

Let no one imagine that he will lose anything of human dignity by this voluntary sell-out of his all to his God. He does not by this degrade himself as a man; rather he finds his right place of high honor as one made in the image of his Creator. His deep disgrace lay in his moral derangement, his unnatural usurpation of the place of God. His honor will be proved by restoring again that stolen throne. In exalting God over all he finds his own highest honor upheld.

Anyone who might feel reluctant to surrender his will to the will of another should remember Jesus' words, "Whosoever committeth sin is the servant of sin." We must of necessity be servant to someone, either to God or to sin. The sinner prides himself on his independence, completely overlooking the fact that he is the weak slave of the sins that rule his members. The man who surrenders to Christ exchanges a cruel slave driver for a kind and gentle Master whose yoke is easy and whose burden is light.

Made as we were in the image of God we scarcely find it strange to take again our God as our All. God was our original habitat and our hearts cannot but feel at home when they enter again that ancient and beautiful abode.

I hope it is clear that there is a logic behind God's claim to pre-eminence. That place is His by every right in earth or heaven. While we take to ourselves the place that is His the whole course of our lives is out of joint. Nothing will or can restore order till our hearts make the great decision: God shall be exalted above.

"Them that honour me I will honour," said God once to a priest of Israel, and that ancient law of the Kingdom stands today unchanged by the passing of time or the changes of dispensation. The whole Bible and every page of history proclaim the perpetuation of that law. "If any man serve me, him will my Father honour," said our Lord Jesus, tying in the old with the new and revealing the essential unity of His ways with men.

Sometimes the best way to see a thing is to look at its opposite. Eli and his sons are placed in the priesthood with the stipulation that they honor God in their lives and ministrations. This they fail to do, and God sends Samuel to announce the consequences. Unknown to Eli this law of reciprocal honor has been all the while secretly working, and now the time has come for judgment to fall. Hophni and Phineas, the degenerate priests, fall in battle, the wife of Hophni dies in childbirth, Israel flees before her enemies, the ark of God is captured by the Philistines and the old man Eli falls backward and dies of a broken neck. Thus stark utter tragedy followed upon Eli's failure to honor God.

Now set over against this almost any Bible character who honestly tried to glorify God in his earthly walk. See how God winked at weaknesses and overlooked failures as He poured upon His servants grace and blessing untold. Let it be Abraham, Jacob, David, Daniel, Elijah or whom you will; honor followed honor as harvest the seed. The man of God set his heart to exalt God above all; God accepted his intention as fact and acted accordingly. Not perfection, but holy intention made the difference.

In our Lord Jesus Christ this law was seen in simple perfection. In His lowly manhood He humbled Himself and gladly gave all glory to His Father in heaven. He sought not His own honor, but the honor of God who sent Him. "If I honour myself," He said on one occasion, "my honour is nothing; it is my Father that honoureth me." So far had the proud Pharisees departed from this law that they could not understand one who honored God at his own expense. "I honour my Father," said Jesus to them, "and ye do dishonour me."

Another saying of Jesus, and a most disturbing one, was put in the form of a question, "How can ye believe, which receive honour one of another, and seek not the honour that cometh from God alone?" If I understand this correctly Christ taught here the alarming doctrine that the desire for honor among men made belief impossible. Is this sin at the root of religious unbelief? Could it be that those "intellectual difficulties" which men blame for their inability to believe are but smoke screens to conceal the real cause that lies behind them? Was it this greedy desire for honor from man that made men into Pharisees and Pharisees into Deicides? Is this the secret back of religious self-righteousness and empty worship? I believe it may be. The whole course of the life is upset by failure to put God where He belongs. We exalt ourselves instead of God and the curse follows.

In our desire after God let us keep always in mind that God also hath desire, and His desire is toward the sons of men, and more particularly toward those sons of men who will make the once-for-all decision to exalt Him over all. Such as these are precious to God above all treasures of earth or sea. In them God finds a theater where He can display His exceeding kindness toward us in Christ Jesus. With them God can walk unhindered, toward them He can act like the God He is.

In speaking thus I have one fear; it is that I may convince the mind before God can win the heart. For this God-above-all position is one not easy to take. The mind may approve it while not having the consent of the will to put it into effect. While the imagination races ahead to honor God, the will may lag behind and the man never guess how divided his heart is. The whole man must make the decision before the heart can know any real satisfaction. God wants us all, and He will not rest till He gets us all. No part of the man will do.

Let us pray over this in detail, throwing ourselves at God's feet and meaning everything we say. No one who prays thus in sincerity need wait long for tokens of divine acceptance. God will unveil His glory before His servant's eyes, and He will place all His treasures at the disposal of such a one, for He knows that His honor is safe in such consecrated hands.

O God, be Thou exalted over my possessions. Nothing of earth's treasures shall seem dear unto me if only Thou art glorified in my life. Be Thou exalted over my friendships. I am determined that Thou shalt be above all, though I must stand deserted and alone in the midst of the earth. Be Thou exalted above my comforts. Though it mean the loss of bodily comforts and the carrying of heavy crosses I shall keep my vow made this day before Thee. Be Thou exalted over my reputation. Make me ambitious to please Thee even if as a result I must sink into obscurity and my name be forgotten as a dream. Rise, O Lord, into Thy proper place of honor, above my ambitions, above my likes and dislikes, above my family, my health and even my life itself. Let me decrease that Thou mayest increase, let me sink that Thou mayest rise above. Ride forth upon me as Thou didst ride into Jerusalem mounted upon the humble little beast, a colt, the foal of an ass, and let me hear the children cry to Thee, "Hosanna in the highest."

Meekness and Rest

Blessed are the meek: for they shall inherit the earth.— Matt. 5:5

A fairly accurate description of the human race might be furnished one unacquainted with it by taking the Beatitudes, turning them wrong side out and saying, "Here is your human race." For the exact opposite of the virtues in the Beatitudes are the very qualities which distinguish human life and conduct.

In the world of men we find nothing approaching the virtues of which Jesus spoke in the opening words of the famous Sermon on the Mount. Instead of poverty of spirit we find the rankest kind of pride; instead of mourners we find pleasure seekers; instead of meekness, arrogance; instead of hunger after righteousness we hear men saying, "I am rich and increased with goods and have need of nothing"; instead of mercy we find cruelty; instead of purity of heart, corrupt imaginings; instead of peacemakers we find men quarrelsome and resentful; instead of rejoicing in mistreatment we find them fighting back with every weapon at their command.

Of this kind of moral stuff civilized society is composed. The atmosphere is charged with it; we breathe it with every breath and drink it with our mother's milk. Culture and education refine these things slightly but leave them basically untouched. A whole world of literature has been created to justify this kind of life as the only normal one. And this is the more to be wondered at seeing that these are the evils which make life the bitter struggle it is for all of us. All our heartaches and a great many of our physical ills spring directly out of our sins. Pride, arrogance, resentfulness, evil imaginings, malice, greed: these are the sources of more human pain than all the diseases that ever afflicted mortal flesh.

Into a world like this the sound of Jesus' words comes wonderful and strange, a visitation from above. It is well that He spoke, for no one else could have done it as well; and it is good that we listen. His words are the essence of truth. He is not offering an opinion; Jesus never uttered opinions. He never guessed; He knew, and He knows. His words are not as Solomon's were, the sum of sound wisdom or the results of keen observation. He spoke out of the fulness of His Godhead, and His words are very Truth itself. He is the only one who could say "blessed" with complete authority, for He is the Blessed One come from the world above to confer blessedness upon mankind. And His words were supported by deeds mightier than any performed on this earth by any other man. It is wisdom for us to listen.

As was often so with Jesus, He used this word "meek" in a brief crisp sentence, and not till some time later did He go on to explain it. In the same book of Matthew He tells us more about it and applies it to our lives. "Come unto me, all ye that labour and are heavy laden, and I will give you rest. Take my yoke upon you, and learn of me; for I am meek and lowly in heart: and ye shall find rest unto your souls. For my yoke is easy, and my burden is light." Here we have two things standing in contrast to each other, a burden and a rest. The burden is not a local one, peculiar to those first hearers, but one which is borne by the whole human race. It consists not of political oppression or poverty or hard work. It is far deeper than that. It is felt by the rich as well as the poor for it is something from which wealth and idleness can never deliver us.

The burden borne by mankind is a heavy and a crushing thing. The word Jesus used means a load carried or toil borne to the point of exhaustion. Rest is simply release from that burden. It is not something we do, it is what comes to us when we cease to do. His own meekness, that is the rest.

Let us examine our burden. It is altogether an interior one. It attacks the heart and the mind and reaches the body only from within. First, there is the burden of pride. The labor of self-love is a heavy one indeed. Think for yourself whether much of your sorrow has not arisen from someone speaking slightingly of you. As long as you set yourself up as a little god to which you must be loyal there will be those who will delight to offer affront to your idol. How then can you hope to have inward peace? The heart's fierce effort to protect itself from every slight, to shield its touchy honor from the bad opinion of friend and enemy, will never let the mind have rest. Continue this fight through the years and the burden will become intolerable. Yet the sons of earth are carrying this burden continually, challenging every word spoken against them, cringing under every criticism, smarting under each fancied slight, tossing sleepless if another is preferred before them.

Such a burden as this is not necessary to bear. Jesus calls us to His rest, and meekness is His method. The meek man cares not at all who is greater than he, for he has long ago decided that the esteem of the world is not worth the effort. He develops toward himself a kindly sense of humor and learns to say, "Oh, so you have been overlooked? They have placed someone else before you? They have whispered that you are pretty small stuff after all? And now you feel hurt because the world is saying about you the very things you have been saying about yourself? Only yesterday you were telling God that you were nothing, a mere worm of the dust. Where is your consistency? Come on, humble yourself, and cease to care what men think."

The meek man is not a human mouse afflicted with a sense of his own inferiority. Rather he may be in his moral life as bold as a lion and as strong as Samson; but he has stopped being fooled about himself. He has accepted God's estimate of his own life. He knows he is as weak and helpless as God has declared him to be, but paradoxically, he knows at the same time that he is in the sight of God of more importance than angels. In himself, nothing; in God, everything. That is his motto. He knows well that the world will never see him as God sees him and he has stopped caring. He rests perfectly content to allow God to place His own values. He will be patient to wait for the day when everything will get its own price tag and real worth will come into its own. Then the righteous shall shine forth in the Kingdom of their Father. He is willing to wait for that day.

In the meantime he will have attained a place of soul rest. As he walks on in meekness he will be happy to let God defend him. The old struggle to defend himself is over. He has found the peace which meekness brings.

Then also he will get deliverance from the burden of pretense. By this I mean not hypocrisy, but the common human desire to put the best foot forward and hide from the world our real inward poverty. For sin has played many evil tricks upon us, and one has been the infusing into us a false sense of shame. There is hardly a man or woman who dares to be just what he or she is without doctoring up the impression. The fear of being found out gnaws like rodents within their hearts. The man of culture is haunted by the fear that he will some day come upon a man more cultured than himself. The learned man fears to meet a man more learned than he. The rich man sweats under the fear that his clothes or his car or his house will sometime be made to look cheap by comparison with those of another rich man. So-called "society" runs by a motivation not higher than this, and the poorer classes on their level are little better.

Let no one smile this off. These burdens are real, and little by little they kill the victims of this evil and unnatural way of life. And the psychology created by years of this kind of thing makes true meekness seem as unreal as a dream, as aloof as a star. To all the victims of the gnawing disease Jesus says, "Ye must become as little children." For little children do not compare; they receive direct enjoyment from what they have without relating it to something else or someone else. Only as they get older and sin begins to stir within their hearts do jealousy and envy appear. Then they are unable to enjoy what they have if someone else has something larger or better. At that early age does the galling burden come down upon their tender souls, and it never leaves them till Jesus sets them free.

Another source of burden is artificiality. I am sure that most people live in secret fear that some day they will be careless and by chance an enemy or friend will be allowed to peep into their poor empty souls. So they are never relaxed. Bright people are tense and alert in fear that they may be trapped into saying something common or stupid. Traveled people are afraid that they may meet some Marco Polo who is able to describe some remote place where they have never been.

This unnatural condition is part of our sad heritage of sin, but in our day it is aggravated by our whole way of life. Advertising is largely based upon this habit of pretense. "Courses" are offered in this or that field of human learning frankly appealing to the victim's desire to shine at a party. Books are sold, clothes and cosmetics are peddled, by playing continually upon this desire to appear what we are not. Artificiality is one curse that will drop away the moment we kneel at Jesus' feet and surrender ourselves to His meekness. Then we will not care what people think of us so long as God is pleased. Then what we are will be everything; what we appear will take its place far down the scale of interest for us. Apart from sin we have nothing of which to be ashamed. Only an evil desire to shine makes us want to appear other than we are.

The heart of the world is breaking under this load of pride and pretense. There is no release from our burden apart from the meekness of Christ. Good keen reasoning may help slightly, but so strong is this vice that if we push it down one place it will come up somewhere else. To men and women everywhere Jesus says, "Come unto me, and I will give you rest." The rest He offers is the rest of meekness, the blessed relief which comes when we accept ourselves for what we are and cease to pretend. It will take some courage at first, but the needed grace will come as we learn that we are sharing this new and easy yoke with the strong Son of God Himself. He calls it "my yoke," and He walks at one end while we walk at the other.

Lord, make me childlike. Deliver me from the urge to compete with another for place or prestige or position. I would be simple and artless as a little child. Deliver me from pose and pretense. Forgive me for thinking of myself. Help me to forget myself and find my true peace in beholding Thee. That Thou mayest answer this prayer I humble myself before Thee. Lay upon me Thy easy yoke of self-forgetfulness that through it I may find rest. Amen.

THE SACRAMENT OF LIVING

*Whether therefore ye eat, or drink,
or whatsoever ye do, do all to the
glory of God.— I Cor. 10:31*

One of the greatest hindrances to internal peace which the Christian encounters is the common habit of dividing our lives into two areas, the sacred and the secular. As these areas are conceived to exist apart from each other and to be morally and spiritually incompatible, and as we are compelled by the necessities of living to be always crossing back and forth from the one to the other, our inner lives tend to break up so that we live a divided instead of a unified life.

Our trouble springs from the fact that we who follow Christ inhabit at once two worlds, the spiritual and the natural. As children of Adam we live our lives on earth subject to the limitations of the flesh and the weaknesses and ills to which human nature is heir. Merely to live among men requires of us years of hard toil and much care and attention to the things of this world. In sharp contrast to this is our life in the Spirit. There we enjoy another and higher kind of life; we are children of God; we possess heavenly status and enjoy intimate fellowship with Christ.

This tends to divide our total life into two departments. We come unconsciously to recognize two sets of actions. The first are performed with a feeling of satisfaction and a firm assurance that they are pleasing to God. These are the sacred acts and they are usually thought to be prayer, Bible reading, hymn singing, church attendance and such other acts as spring directly from faith. They may be known by the fact that they have no direct relation to this world, and would have no meaning whatever except as faith shows us another world, "an house not made with hands, eternal in the heavens."

Over against these sacred acts are the secular ones. They include all of the ordinary activities of life which we share with the sons and daughters of Adam: eating, sleeping, working, looking after the needs of the body and performing our dull and prosaic duties here on earth. These we often do reluctantly and with many misgivings, often apologizing to God for what we consider a waste of time and strength. The upshot of this is that we are uneasy most of the time. We go about our common tasks with a feeling of deep frustration, telling ourselves pensively that there's a better day coming when we shall slough off this earthly shell and be bothered no more with the affairs of this world.

This is the old sacred-secular antithesis. Most Christians are caught in its trap. They cannot get a satisfactory adjustment between the claims of the two worlds. They try to walk the tight rope between two kingdoms and they find no peace in either. Their strength is reduced, their outlook confused and their joy taken from them.

I believe this state of affairs to be wholly unnecessary. We have gotten ourselves on the horns of a dilemma, true enough, but the dilemma is not real. It is a creature of misunderstanding. The sacred-secular antithesis has no foundation in the New Testament. Without doubt a more perfect understanding of Christian truth will deliver us from it.

The Lord Jesus Christ Himself is our perfect example, and He knew no divided life. In the Presence of His Father He lived on earth without strain from babyhood to His death on the cross. God accepted the offering of His total life, and made no distinction between act and act. "I do always the things that please him," was His brief summary of His own life as it related to the Father. As He moved among men He was poised and restful. What pressure and suffering He endured grew out of His position as the world's sin bearer; they were never the result of moral uncertainty or spiritual maladjustment.

Paul's exhortation to "do all to the glory of God" is more than pious idealism. It is an integral part of the sacred revelation and is to be accepted as the very Word of Truth. It opens before us the possibility of making every act of our lives contribute to the glory of God. Lest we should be too timid to include everything, Paul mentions specifically eating and drinking. This humble privilege we share with the beasts that perish. If these lowly animal acts can be so performed as to honor God, then it becomes difficult to conceive of one that cannot.

That monkish hatred of the body which figures so prominently in the works of certain early devotional writers is wholly without support in the Word of God. Common modesty is found in the Sacred Scriptures, it is true, but never prudery or a false sense of shame. The New Testament accepts as a matter of course that in His incarnation our Lord took upon Him a real human body, and no effort is made to steer around the downright implications of such a fact. He lived in that body here among men and never once performed a non-sacred act. His presence in human flesh sweeps away forever the evil notion that there is about the human body something innately offensive to the Deity. God created our bodies, and we do not offend Him by placing the responsibility where it belongs. He is not ashamed of the work of His own hands.

Perversion, misuse and abuse of our human powers should give us cause enough to be ashamed. Bodily acts done in sin and contrary to nature can never honor God. Wherever the human will introduces moral evil we have no longer our innocent and harmless powers as God made them; we have instead an abused and twisted thing which can never bring glory to its Creator.

Let us, however, assume that perversion and abuse are not present. Let us think of a Christian believer in whose life the twin wonders of repentance and the new birth have been wrought. He is now living according to the will of God as he understands it from the written Word. Of such a one it may be said that every act of his life is or can be as truly sacred as prayer or baptism or the Lord's Supper. To say this is not to bring all acts down to one dead level; it is rather to lift every act up into a living kingdom and turn the whole life into a sacrament.

If a sacrament is an external expression of an inward grace than we need not hesitate to accept the above thesis. By one act of consecration of our total selves to God we can make every subsequent act express that consecration. We need no more be ashamed of our body—the fleshly servant that carries us through life— than Jesus was of the humble beast upon which He rode into Jerusalem. "The Lord hath need of him" may well apply to our mortal bodies. If Christ dwells in us we may bear about the Lord of glory as the little beast did of old and give occasion to the multitudes to cry, "Hosanna in the highest."

That we see this truth is not enough. If we would escape from the toils of the sacred-secular dilemma the truth must "run in our blood" and condition the complexion of our thoughts. We must practice living to the glory of God, actually and determinedly. By meditation upon this truth, by talking it over with God often in our prayers, by recalling it to our minds frequently as we move about among men, a sense of its wondrous meaning will begin to take hold of us. The old painful duality will go down before a restful unity of life. The knowledge that we are all God's, that He has received all and rejected nothing, will unify our inner lives and make everything sacred to us.

This is not quite all. Long-held habits do not die easily. It will take intelligent thought and a great deal of reverent prayer to escape completely from the sacred-secular psychology. For instance it may be difficult for the average Christian to get hold of the idea that his daily labors can be performed as acts of worship acceptable to God by Jesus Christ. The old antithesis will crop up in the back of his head sometimes to disturb his peace of mind. Nor will that old serpent the devil take all this lying down. He will be there in the cab or at the desk or in the field to remind the Christian that he is giving the better part of his day to the things of this world and allotting to his religious duties only a trifling portion of his time. And unless great care is taken this will create confusion and bring discouragement and heaviness of heart.

We can meet this successfully only by the exercise of an aggressive faith. We must offer all our acts to God and believe that He accepts them. Then hold firmly to that position and keep insisting that every act of every hour of the day and night be included in the transaction. Keep reminding God in our times of private prayer that we mean every act for His glory; then supplement those times by a thousand thought-prayers as we go about the job of living. Let us practice the fine art of making every work a priestly ministration. Let us believe that God is in all our simple deeds and learn to find Him there.

A concomitant of the error which we have been discussing is the sacred-secular antithesis as applied to places. It is little short of astonishing that we can read the New Testament and still believe in the inherent sacredness of places as distinguished from other places. This error is so widespread that one feels all alone when he tries to combat it. It has acted as a kind of dye to color the thinking of religious persons and has colored the eyes as well so that it is all but impossible to detect its fallacy. In the face of every New Testament teaching to the contrary it has been said and sung throughout the centuries and accepted as a part of the Christian message, the which it most surely is not. Only the Quakers, so far as my knowledge goes, have had the perception to see the error and the courage to expose it.

Here are the facts as I see them. For four hundred years Israel had dwelt in Egypt, surrounded by the crassest idolatry. By the hand of Moses they were brought out at last and started toward the land of promise. The very idea of holiness had been lost to them. To correct this, God began at the bottom. He localized Himself in the cloud and fire and later when the tabernacle had been built He dwelt in fiery manifestation in the Holy of Holies. By innumerable distinctions God taught Israel the difference between holy and unholy. There were holy days, holy vessels, holy garments. There were washings, sacrifices, offerings of many kinds. By these means Israel learned that God is holy. It was this that He was teaching them. Not the holiness of things or places, but the holiness of Jehovah was the lesson they must learn.

Then came the great day when Christ appeared. Immediately He began to say, "Ye have heard that it was said by them of old time—but I say unto you." The Old Testament schooling was over. When Christ died on the cross the veil of the temple was rent from top to bottom. The Holy of Holies was opened to everyone who would enter in faith. Christ's words were remembered, "The hour cometh, when ye shall neither in this mountain, nor yet at Jerusalem, worship the Father. . . . But the hour cometh, and now is, when the true worshippers shall worship the Father in spirit and in truth: for the Father seeketh such to worship Him. God is Spirit, and they that worship him must worship him in spirit and in truth."

Shortly after, Paul took up the cry of liberty and declared all meats clean, every day holy, all places sacred and every act acceptable to God. The sacredness of times and places, a half-light necessary to the education of the race, passed away before the full sun of spiritual worship.

The essential spirituality of worship remained the possession of the Church until it was slowly lost with the passing of the years. Then the natural legality of the fallen hearts of men began to introduce the old distinctions. The Church came to observe again days and seasons and times. Certain places were chosen and marked out as holy in a special sense. Differences were observed between one and another day or place or person. "The sacraments" were first two, then three, then four until with the triumph of Romanism they were fixed at seven.

In all charity, and with no desire to reflect unkindly upon any Christian, however misled, I would point out that the Roman Catholic church represents today the sacred-secular heresy carried to its logical conclusion. Its deadliest effect is the complete cleavage it introduces between religion and life. Its teachers attempt to avoid this snare by many footnotes and multitudinous explanations, but the mind's instinct for logic is too strong. In practical living the cleavage is a fact.

From this bondage reformers and puritans and mystics have labored to free us. Today the trend in conservative circles is back toward that bondage again. It is said that a horse after it has been led out of a burning building will sometimes by a strange obstinacy break loose from its rescuer and dash back into the building again to perish in the flame. By some such stubborn tendency toward error Fundamentalism in our day is moving back toward spiritual slavery. The observation of days and times is becoming more and more prominent among us. "Lent" and "holy week" and "good" Friday are words heard more and more frequently upon the lips of gospel Christians. We do not know when we are well off.

In order that I may be understood and not be misunderstood I would throw into relief the practical implications of the teaching for which I have been arguing, i.e., the sacramental quality of every day living. Over against its positive meanings I should like to point out a few things it does not mean.

It does not mean, for instance, that everything we do is of equal importance with everything else we do or may do. One act of a good man's life may differ widely from another in importance. Paul's sewing of tents was not equal to his writing of an Epistle to the Romans, but both were accepted of God and both were true acts of worship. Certainly it is more important to lead a soul to Christ than to plant a garden, but the planting of the garden can be as holy an act as the winning of a soul.

Again, it does not mean that every man is as useful as every other man. Gifts differ in the body of Christ. A Billy Bray is not to be compared with a Luther or a Wesley for sheer usefulness to the Church and to the world; but the service of the less gifted brother is as pure as that of the more gifted, and God accepts both with equal pleasure.

The "layman" need never think of his humbler task as being inferior to that of his minister. Let every man abide in the calling wherein he is called and his work will be as sacred as the work of the ministry. It is not what a man does that determines whether his work is sacred or secular, it is why he does it. The motive is everything. Let a man sanctify the Lord God in his heart and he can thereafter do no common act. All he does is good and acceptable to God through Jesus Christ. For such a man, living itself will be sacramental and the whole world a sanctuary. His entire life will be a priestly ministration. As he performs his never so simple task he will hear the voice of the seraphim saying, "Holy, Holy, Holy, is the Lord of hosts: the whole earth is full of his glory."

Lord, I would trust Thee completely; I would be altogether Thine; I would exalt Thee above all. I desire that I may feel no sense of possessing anything outside of Thee. I want constantly to be aware of Thy overshadowing Presence and to hear Thy speaking Voice. I long to live in restful sincerity of heart. I want to live so fully in the Spirit that all my thought may be as sweet incense ascending to Thee and every act of my life may be an act of worship. Therefore I pray in the words of Thy great servant of old, "I beseech Thee so for to cleanse the intent of mine heart with the unspeakable gift of Thy grace, that I may perfectly love Thee and worthily praise Thee." And all this I confidently believe Thou wilt grant me through the merits of Jesus Christ Thy Son. Amen.

Keys

to the

Deeper Life

[1957]

No Revival Without Reformation

Wherever Christians meet these days one word is sure to be heard constantly repeated; that word is revival.

In sermon, song and prayer we are forever reminding the Lord and each other that what we must have to solve all our spiritual problems is a "mighty, old-time revival." The religious press, too, has largely gone over to the proposition that revival is the one great need of the hour, and anyone who is capable of preparing a brief for revival is sure to find many editors who will publish it.

So strongly is the breeze blowing for revival that scarcely anyone appears to have the discernment or the courage to turn around and lean into the wind, even though the truth may easily lie in that direction. Religion has its vogues very much as do philosophy, politics and women's fashions. Historically the major world religions have had their periods of decline and recovery, and those recoveries are bluntly called revivals by the annalists.

Let us not forget that in some lands Islam is now enjoying a revival, and the latest report from Japan indicates that after a brief eclipse following World War II Shintoism is making a remarkable come-back. In our own country Roman Catholicism as well as liberal Protestantism is moving forward at such a rate that the word revival is almost necessary to describe the phenomenon. And this without any perceptible elevation of the moral standards of its devotees.

A religion, even popular Christianity, could enjoy a boom altogether divorced from the transforming power of the Holy Spirit and so leave the church of the next generation worse off than it would have been if the boom had never occurred. I believe that the imperative need of the day is not simply revival, but a radical reformation that will go to the root of our moral and spiritual maladies and deal with causes rather than with consequences, with the disease rather than with symptoms.

It is my considered opinion that under the present circumstances we do not want revival at all. A widespread revival of the kind of

Christianity we know today in America might prove to be a moral tragedy from which we would not recover in a hundred years.

Here are my reasons. A generation ago, as a reaction from Higher Criticism and its offspring, Modernism, there arose in Protestantism a powerful movement in defense of the historic Christian faith. This, for obvious reasons, came to be known as Fundamentalism. It was a more or less spontaneous movement without much organization, but its purpose wherever it appeared was the same: to stay "the rising tide of negation" in Christian theology and to restate and defend the basic doctrines of New Testament Christianity. This much is history.

Falls Victim To Its Virtues

What is generally overlooked is that Fundamentalism, as it spread throughout the various denominations and non-denominational groups, fell victim to its own virtues. The Word died in the hands of its friends. Verbal inspiration, for instance (a doctrine which I have always held and do now hold), soon became afflicted with rigor mortis. The voice of the prophet was silenced and the scribe captured the minds of the faithful. In large areas the religious imagination withered. An unofficial hierarchy decided what Christians were to believe. Not the Scriptures, but what the scribe thought the Scriptures meant became the Christian creed. Christian colleges, seminaries, Bible institutes, Bible conferences, popular Bible expositors all joined to promote the cult of textualism. The system of extreme dispensationalism which was devised, relieved the Christian of repentance, obedience and cross-carrying in any other than the most formal sense. Whole sections of the New Testament were taken from the Church and disposed of after a rigid system of "dividing the Word of truth."

All this resulted in a religious mentality inimical to the true faith of Christ. A kind of cold mist settled over Fundamentalism. Below, the terrain was familiar. This was New Testament Christianity, to be sure. The basic doctrines of the Bible were there, but the climate was just not favorable to the sweet fruits of the Spirit.

The whole mood was different from that of the Early Church and of the great souls who suffered and sang and worshiped in the centuries past. The doctrines were sound but something vital was missing. The tree of correct doctrine was never allowed to blossom. The voice of the turtle [dove] was rarely heard in the land; instead, the parrot sat on his artificial perch and dutifully repeated what he had been taught and the whole emotional tone was somber and dull. Faith, a mighty, vitalizing doctrine in the mouths of the apostles, became in the mouth of the scribe another thing altogether and power went from it. As the letter triumphed, the Spirit withdrew and textualism ruled supreme. It was the time of the believer's Babylonian captivity.

In the interest of accuracy it should be said that this was a general condition only. Certainly there were some even in those low times whose longing hearts were better theologians than their teachers were. These pressed on to a fullness and power unknown to the rest. But they were not many and the odds were too great; they could not dispel the mist that hung over the land.

The error of textualism is not doctrinal. It is far more subtle than that and much more difficult to discover, but its effects are just as deadly. Not its theological beliefs are at fault, but its assumptions.

It assumes, for instance, that if we have the word for a thing we have the thing itself. If it is in the Bible, it is in us. If we have the doctrine, we have the experience. If something was true of Paul it is of necessity true of us because we accept Paul's epistles as divinely inspired. The Bible tells us how to be saved, but textualism goes on to make it tell us that we are saved, something which in the very nature of things it cannot do. Assurance of individual salvation is thus no more than a logical conclusion drawn from doctrinal premises, and the resultant experience wholly mental.

Revolt From Mental Tyranny

Then came the revolt. The human mind can endure textualism just so long before it seeks a way of escape. So, quietly and quite unaware that any revolt was taking place, the masses of Fundamentalism reacted, not from the teaching of the Bible but from the mental tyranny of the scribes. With the recklessness of drowning men they fought their way up for air and struck out blindly for greater freedom of thought and for the emotional satisfaction their natures demanded and their teachers denied them.

The result over the last 20 years has been a religious debauch hardly equaled since Israel worshiped the golden calf. Of us Bible Christians it may truthfully be said that we "sat down to eat and to drink, and rose up to play." The separating line between the Church and the world has been all but obliterated.

Aside from a few of the grosser sins, the sins of the unregenerated world are now approved by a shocking number of professedly "born-again" Christians, and copied eagerly. Young Christians take as their models the rankest kind of worldlings and try to be as much like them as possible. Religious leaders have adopted the techniques of the advertisers; boasting, baiting and shameless exaggerating are now carried on as a normal procedure in church work. The moral climate is not that of the New Testament, but that of Hollywood and Broadway.

Most evangelicals no longer initiate; they imitate, and the world is their model. The holy faith of our fathers has in many places been made a form of entertainment, and the appalling thing is that all this has been fed down to the masses from the top.

That note of protest which began with the New Testament and which was always heard loudest when the Church was most powerful has been successfully silenced. The radical element in testimony and life that once made Christians hated by the world is missing from present-day evangelicalism. Christians were once revolutionists—moral, not political—but we have lost our revolutionary character. It is no longer either dangerous or costly to be a Christian. Grace has become not free, but cheap. We are busy these days proving to the world that they can have all the benefits of the Gospel without any inconvenience to their customary way of life. It's "all this, and heaven too."

This description of modern Christianity, while not universally applicable, is yet true of an overwhelming majority of present-day Christians. For this reason it is useless for large companies of believers to spend long hours begging God to send revival. Unless we intend to reform we may as well not pray. Unless praying men have the insight and faith to amend their whole way of life to conform to the New Testament pattern there can be no true revival.

When Praying Is Wrong

Sometimes praying is not only useless, it is wrong. Here is an example: Israel had been defeated at Ai, and "Joshua rent his clothes, and fell to the earth upon his face before the ark of the Lord until the eventide, he and the elders of Israel, and put dust upon their heads."

According to our modern philosophy of revival this was the thing to do and, if continued long enough, should certainly have persuaded God and brought the blessing. But "the Lord said unto Joshua, Get thee up; wherefore liest thou upon thy face? Israel hath sinned, and they have also transgressed my covenant which I commanded them . . . Up, sanctify the people, and say, Sanctify yourselves against tomorrow; for thus saith the Lord God of Israel. There is an accursed thing in the midst of thee, O Israel: thou canst not stand before thine enemies, until ye take away the accursed thing from among you."

We must have a reformation within the Church. To beg for a flood of blessing to come upon a backslidden and disobedient Church is to waste time and effort. A new wave of religious interest will do no more than add numbers to churches that have no intention to own the Lordship of Jesus and come under obedience to His commandments. God is not interested in increased church attendance unless those who attend amend their ways and begin to live holy lives.

Once the Lord through the mouth of the prophet Isaiah said a word that should settle this thing forever: "To what purpose is the multitude of your sacrifices unto me? saith the Lord: I am full of the burnt-offerings of rams, and the fat of fed beasts; and I delight not in the blood of bullocks, or of lambs, or of he goats. When ye come to appear before me, who hath required this at your hand, to tread my courts? Bring no more vain oblations; incense is an abomination unto me; the new moons and sabbaths, the calling of assemblies, I cannot away with; it is iniquity, even the solemn meeting . . . Wash you, make you clean; put away the evil of your doings from before mine eyes; cease to do evil; learn to do well; seek judgment, relieve the oppressed, judge the fatherless, plead for the widow . . . If ye be willing and obedient, ye shall eat the good of the land."

Prayer for revival will prevail when it is accompanied by radical amendment of life; not before. All-night prayer meetings that are not preceded by practical repentance may actually be displeasing to God. "To obey is better than sacrifice."

We must return to New Testament Christianity, not in creed only but in complete manner of life as well. Separation, obedience, humility, simplicity, gravity, self-control, modesty, cross-bearing: these all must again be made a living part of the total Christian concept and be carried out in everyday conduct. We must cleanse the temple of the hucksters and the money changers and come fully under the authority of our risen Lord once more. And this applies to this writer and to this magazine as well as to everyone that names the name of Jesus. Then we can pray with confidence and expect true revival to follow.

The Deeper Life: What is it?

Suppose some angelic being who had since creation known the deep, still rapture of dwelling in the divine Presence would appear on earth and live awhile among us Christians. Don't you imagine he might be astonished at what he saw?

He might, for instance, wonder how we can be contented with our poor, commonplace level of spiritual experience. In our hands, after all, is a message from God not only inviting us into His holy fellowship but also giving us detailed instructions about how to get there. After feasting on the bliss of intimate communion with God how could such a being understand the casual, easily satisfied spirit which characterizes most evangelicals today? And if our hypothetical being knew such blazing souls as Moses, David, Isaiah, Paul, John, Stephen, Augustine, Rolle, Rutherford, Newton, Brainerd and Faber, he might logically conclude that 20th century Christians had misunderstood some vital doctrine of the faith somewhere and had stopped short of a true acquaintance with God.

What if he sat in on the daily sessions of an average Bible conference and noted the extravagant claims, we Christians make for ourselves as believers in Christ and compared them with our actual spiritual experiences? He would surely conclude that there was a serious contradiction between what we think we are and what we are in reality. The bold claims that we are sons of God, that we are risen with Christ and seated with Him in heavenly places, that we are indwelt by the life-giving Spirit, that we are members of the Body of Christ and children of the new creation, are negated by our attitudes, our behavior and, most of all, by our lack of fervor and by the absence of a spirit of worship within us.

Perhaps if our heavenly visitor pointed out the great disparity between our doctrinal beliefs and our lives, he might be dismissed with a smiling explanation that it is but the normal difference between our sure standing and our variable state. Certainly then, he would be appalled that as beings once made in the image of God we could allow ourselves thus to play with words and trifle with our own souls.

Significant, isn't it, that of all who hold the evangelical position those Christians who lay the greatest store by Paul are often the least Pauline in spirit. There is a vast and important difference between a Pauline creed and a Pauline life. Some of us who have for years sympathetically observed the Christian scene feel constrained to paraphrase the words of the dying queen and cry out, "O Paul! Paul! what evils have been committed in thy name." Tens of thousands of believers who pride themselves on their understanding of Romans and Ephesians cannot conceal the sharp spiritual contradiction that exists between their hearts and the heart of Paul.

That difference may be stated this way: Paul was a seeker and a finder and a seeker still. They seek and find and seek no more. After "accepting" Christ they tend to substitute logic for life and doctrine for experience.

For them the truth becomes a veil to hide the face of God; for Paul it was a door into His very Presence. Paul's spirit was that of the loving explorer. He was a prospector among the hills of God searching for the gold of personal spiritual acquaintance. Many today stand by Paul's doctrine who will not follow him in his passionate yearning for divine reality. Can these be said to be Pauline in any but the most nominal sense?

If Paul Were Preaching Today

With the words "That I may know him" Paul answered the whining claims of the flesh and raced on toward perfection. All gain he counted loss for the excellency of the knowledge of Christ Jesus the Lord, and if to know Him better meant suffering or even death it was all one to Paul. To him conformity to Christ was cheap at any price. He panted after God as the heart pants after the waterbrook, and calm reason had little to do with the way he felt.

Indeed a score of cautious and ignoble excuses might have been advanced to slow him down, and we have heard them all. "Watch out for your health," a prudent friend warns. "There is danger that you become mentally unbalanced," says another. "You'll get a reputation for being an extremist," cries a third, and a sober Bible teacher with more theology than thirst hurries to assure him that there is nothing more to seek. "You are accepted in the beloved," he says, "and blessed with all spiritual blessings in heavenly places in Christ. What more do you want? You have only to believe and to wait for the day of His triumph."

So Paul would be exhorted if he lived among us today, for so in substance have I heard the holy aspirations of the saints damped down and smothered as they leaped up to meet God in an increasing degree of intimacy. But knowing Paul as we do, it is safe to assume that he would ignore this low counsel of expediency and press onward toward the mark for the prize of the high calling of God in Christ Jesus. And we do well to follow him.

When the apostle cries "That I may know him," he uses the word know not in its intellectual but in its experiential sense. We must look for the meaning—not to the mind but to the heart. Theological knowledge is knowledge about God. While this is indispensable it is not sufficient. It bears the same relation to man's spiritual need as a well does to the need of his physical body. It is not the rock-lined pit for which the dusty traveler longs, but the sweet, cool water that flows up from it. It is not intellectual knowledge about God that quenches man's ancient heart-thirst, but the very Person and Presence of God Himself. These come to us through Christian doctrine, but they are more than doctrine. Christian truth is designed to lead us to God, not to serve as a substitute for God.

A New Yearning Among Evangelicals

Within the hearts of a growing number of evangelicals in recent days has arisen a new yearning after an above-average spiritual experience. Yet the greater number still shy away from it and raise objections that evidence misunderstanding or fear or plain unbelief. They point to the neurotic, the psychotic, the pseudo-Christian cultist and the intemperate fanatic, and lump them all together without discrimination as followers of the "deeper life."

While this is of course completely preposterous, the fact that such confusion exists obliges those who advocate the Spirit-filled life to define their terms and explain their position. Just what, then, do we mean? And what are we advocating?

For myself, I am reverently concerned that I teach nothing but Christ crucified. For me to accept a teaching or even an emphasis, I must be persuaded that it is scriptural and altogether apostolic in spirit and temper. And it must be in full harmony with the best in the historic church and in the tradition marked by the finest devotional works, the sweetest and most radiant hymnody and the loftiest experiences revealed in Christian biography.

It must lie within the pattern of truth that gave us such saintly souls as Bernard of Clairvaux, John of the Cross, Molinos, Nicholas of Cusa, John Fletcher, David Brainerd, Reginald Heber, Evan Roberts, General Booth and a host of other like souls who, while they were less gifted and lesser known, constitute what Dr. Paul S. Rees (in another context) calls "the seed of survival." And his term is apt, for it was such extraordinary Christians as these who saved Christianity from collapsing under the sheer weight of the spiritual mediocrity it was compelled to carry.

To speak of the "deeper life" is not to speak of anything deeper than simple New Testament religion. Rather it is to insist that believers explore the depths of the Christian evangel for those riches it surely contains but which we are as surely missing. The "deeper life" is deeper only because the average Christian life is tragically shallow.

They who advocate the deeper life today might compare unfavorably with almost any of the Christians that surrounded Paul or Peter in early times. While they may not as yet have made much progress, their faces are toward the light and they are beckoning us on. It is hard to see how we can justify our refusal to heed their call.

What the deeper life advocates are telling us is that we should press on to enjoy in personal inward experience the exalted privileges that are ours in Christ Jesus; that we should insist upon tasting the sweetness of internal worship in spirit as well as in truth; that to reach this ideal we should if necessary push beyond our contented brethren and bring upon ourselves whatever opposition may follow as a result.

The author of the celebrated devotional work, The Cloud of Unknowing, begins his little book with a prayer that expresses the spirit of the deeper life teaching: "God, unto whom all hearts be open . . . and unto whom no secret thing is hid, I beseech Thee so for to cleanse the intent of mine heart with the unspeakable gift of Thy grace, that I may perfectly love Thee and worthily praise Thee. Amen."

Who that is truly born of the Spirit, unless he has been prejudiced by wrong teaching, can object to such a thorough cleansing of the heart as will enable him perfectly to love God and worthily to praise Him? Yet this is exactly what we mean when we speak about the "deeper life" experience. Only we mean that it should be literally fulfilled within the heart, not merely accepted by the head.

Nicephorus, a father of the Eastern Church, in a little treatise on the Spirit-filled life, begins with a call that sounds strange to us only because we have been for so long accustomed to following Jesus afar off and to living among a people that follow Him afar off. "You, who desire to capture the wondrous divine illumination of our Savior Jesus Christ—who seek to feel the divine fire in your heart —who strive to sense and experience the feeling of reconciliation with God—who, in order to unearth the treasure buried in the field of your heart and to gain possession of it, have renounced everything worldly—who desire the candles of your souls to burn brightly even now, and who for this purpose have renounced all the world—who wish by conscious experience to know and to receive the kingdom of heaven existing within you—come and I will impart to you the science of eternal heavenly life—"

Such quotations as these might easily be multiplied till they filled half a dozen volumes. This yearning after God has never completely died in any generation. Always there were some who scorned the low paths and insisted upon walking the high road of spiritual perfection. Yet, strangely enough, that word perfection never meant a spiritual terminal point nor a state of purity that made watchfulness and prayer unnecessary. Exactly the opposite was true.

Hearing But Not Obeying

It has been the unanimous testimony of the greatest Christian souls that the nearer they drew to God the more acute became their consciousness of sin and their sense of personal unworthiness. The purest souls never knew how pure they were and the greatest saints never guessed that they were great. The very thought that they were good or great would have been rejected by them as a temptation of the devil.

They were so engrossed with gazing upon the face of God that they spent scarce a moment looking at themselves. They were suspended in that sweet paradox of spiritual awareness where they knew that they were clean through the blood of the Lamb and yet felt that they deserved only death and hell as their just reward. This feeling is strong in the writings of Paul and is found also in almost all devotional books and among the greatest and most loved hymns.

The quality of evangelical Christianity must be greatly improved if the present unusual interest in religion is not to leave the church worse off than she was before the phenomenon emerged. If we listen I believe we will hear the Lord say to us what He once said to Joshua, "Arise, go over this Jordan, thou, and all this people, unto the and which I do give to them, even to the children of Israel." Or we will hear the writer to the Hebrews say, "Therefore, leaving the first principles of the doctrine of Christ, let us go on unto perfection." And surely we will hear Paul exhort us to "be filled with the Spirit."

If we are alert enough to hear God's voice we must not content ourselves with merely "believing" it. How can any man believe a command? Commands are to be obeyed, and until we have obeyed them we have done exactly nothing at all about them. And to have heard them and not obeyed them is infinitely worse than never to have heard them at all, especially in the light of Christ's soon return and the judgment to come.

GIFTS OF THE SPIRIT: ARE THEY FOR US TODAY?

"Concerning spiritual gifts, brethren," wrote Paul to the Corinthians, "I would not have you ignorant."

Certainly, Paul meant nothing derogatory by this. Rather, he was expressing a charitable concern that his fellow believers should be neither uninformed nor in error about a truth so vastly important as this one.

For some time, it has been evident that we evangelicals have been failing to avail ourselves of the deeper riches of grace that lie in the purposes of God for us. As a consequence, we have been suffering greatly, even tragically. One blessed treasure we have missed is the right to possess the gifts of the Spirit as set forth in such fullness and clarity in the New Testament.

Before proceeding further, however, I want to make it plain that I have had no change of mind about the matter. What I write here has been my faith for many years. No recent spiritual experience has altered my beliefs in any way. I merely bring together truths which I have held during my entire public ministry and have preached with a fair degree of consistency where and when I felt my hearers could receive them.

In their attitude toward the gifts of the Spirit Christians over the last few years have tended to divide themselves into three groups.

First, there are those who magnify the gifts of the Spirit until they can see little else.

Second, there are those who deny that the gifts of the Spirit are intended for the Church in this period of her history.

Third, there are those who appear to be thoroughly bored with the whole thing and do not care to discuss it.

More recently we have become aware of another group, so few in number as scarcely to call for classification. It consists of those who want to know the truth about the Spirit's gifts and to experience whatever God has for them within the context of sound New Testament faith. It is for these that this is written.

What Is The True Church?

Every spiritual problem is at bottom theological. Its solution will depend upon the teaching of the Holy Scriptures plus a correct understanding of that teaching. That correct understanding constitutes a spiritual philosophy, that is, a viewpoint, a high vantage ground from which the whole landscape may be seen at once, each detail appearing in its proper relation to everything else. Once such vantage ground is gained, we are in a position to evaluate any teaching or interpretation that is offered us in the name of truth.

A proper understanding of the gifts of the Spirit in the Church must depend upon a right concept of the nature of the Church. The gift problem cannot be isolated from the larger question and settled by itself.

The true Church is a spiritual phenomenon appearing in human society and intermingling with it to some degree but differing from it sharply in certain vital characteristics. It is composed of regenerated persons who differ from other human beings in that they have a superior kind of life imparted to them at the time of their inward renewal.

They are children of God in a sense not true of any other created beings.

Their origin is divine and their citizenship is in heaven.

They worship God in the Spirit, rejoice in Jesus Christ and have no confidence in the flesh.

They constitute a chosen generation, a royal priesthood, a holy nation, a peculiar people.

They have espoused the cause of a rejected and crucified Man Who claimed to be God and Who has pledged His sacred honor that He will prepare a place for them in His Father's house and return again to conduct them there with rejoicing.

In the meantime they carry His cross, suffer whatever indignities men may heap upon them for His sake, act as His ambassadors and do good to all men in His name.

They steadfastly believe that they will share His triumph, and for this reason they are perfectly willing to share His rejection by a society that does not understand them.

And they have no hard feelings—only charity and compassion and a strong desire that all men may come to repentance and be reconciled to God.

This is a fair summary of one aspect of New Testament teaching about the Church. But another truth more revealing and significant to those seeking information about the gifts of the Spirit is that the

Church is a spiritual body, an organic entity united by the life that dwells within it.

Each Member Joined Together

Each member is joined to the whole by a relationship of life. As a man's soul may be said to be the life of his body, so the indwelling Spirit is the life of the Church.

The idea that the Church is the body of Christ is not an erroneous one, resulting from the pressing too far of a mere figure of speech. The apostle Paul in three of his epistles sets forth this truth in such sobriety of tone and fullness of detail as to preclude the notion that he is employing a casual figure of speech not intended to be taken too literally.

The clear, emphatic teaching of the great apostle is that Christ is the Head of the Church which is His body. The parallel is drawn carefully and continued through long passages. Conclusions are drawn from the doctrine and certain moral conduct is made to depend upon it.

As a normal man consists of a body with various obedient members with a head to direct them, so the true Church is a body, individual Christians being the members and Christ the Head.

The mind works through the members of the body, using them to fulfill its intelligent purposes. Paul speaks of the foot, the hand, the ear, the eye as being members of the body, each with its proper but limited function; but it is the Spirit the worketh in them (I Cor. 12:1-31).

The teaching that the Church is the body of Christ in I Corinthians 12 follows a listing of certain spiritual gifts and reveals the necessity for those gifts.

The intelligent head can work only as it has at its command organs designed for various tasks. It is the mind that sees, but it must have an eye to see through. It is the mind that hears, but it cannot hear without an ear.

And so with all the varied members which are the instruments by means of which the mind moves into the external world to carry out its plans.

As all man's work is done by his mind, so the work of the Church is done by the Spirit, and by Him alone. But to work He must set in the body certain members with abilities specifically created to act as media through which the Spirit can flow toward ordained ends. That in brief is the philosophy of the gifts of the Spirit.

How Many Gifts?

It is usually said that there are nine gifts of the Spirit. (I suppose because Paul lists nine in I Corinthians 12.) Actually, Paul mentions no less than 17 (I Cor. 12:4-11, 27-31; Rom. 12:3-8; Eph. 4:7-11). And these are not natural talents merely, but gifts imparted by the Holy Spirit to fit the believer for his place in the body of Christ. They are like pipes on a great organ, permitting the musician wide scope and range to produce music of the finest quality. But they are, I repeat, more than talents. They are spiritual gifts.

Natural talents enable a man to work within the field of nature; but through the body of Christ God is doing an eternal work above and beyond the realm of fallen nature. This requires supernatural working.

Religious work can be done by natural men without the gifts of the Spirit, and it can be done well and skillfully. But work designed for eternity can only be done by the eternal Spirit. No work has eternity in it unless it is done by the Spirit through gifts He has Himself implanted in the souls of redeemed men.

For a generation certain evangelical teachers have told us that the gifts of the Spirit ceased at the death of the apostles or at the completion of the New Testament. This, of course, is a doctrine without a syllable of biblical authority back of it. Its advocates must accept full responsibility for thus manipulating the Word of God.

The result of this erroneous teaching is that spiritually gifted persons are ominously few among us. When we so desperately need leaders with the gift of discernment, for instance, we do not have them and are compelled to fall back upon the techniques of the world.

This frightening hour calls aloud for men with the gift of prophetic insight. Instead we have men who conduct surveys, polls and panel discussions.

We need men with the gift of knowledge. In their place we have men with scholarship—nothing more.

Thus we may be preparing ourselves for the tragic hour when God may set us aside as so-called evangelicals and raise up another movement to keep New Testament Christianity alive in the earth. Say not, "We be children of Abraham. God is able of these stones to raise up children unto Abraham."

The truth of the matter is that the Scriptures plainly imply the imperative of possessing the gifts of the Spirit. Paul urges that we both "covet" and "desire" spiritual gifts (I Cor. 12:31, I Cor. 14:1). It does not appear to be an optional matter with us but rather a scriptural mandate to those who have been filled with the Spirit.

But I must also add a word of caution.

The various spiritual gifts are not equally valuable, as Paul so carefully explained.

Certain brethren have magnified one gift out of 17 out of all proportion. Among these brethren there have been and are many godly souls, but the general moral results of this teaching have nevertheless not been good.

In practice it has resulted in much shameless exhibitionism, a tendency to depend upon experiences instead of upon Christ and often a lack of ability to distinguish the works of the flesh from the operations of the Spirit.

Those who deny that the gifts are for us today and those who insist upon making a hobby of one gift are both wrong, and we are all suffering the consequence of their error.

Today there is no reason for our remaining longer in doubt. We have every right to expect our Lord to grant to His Church the spiritual gifts which He has never in fact taken away from us, but which we are failing to receive only because of our error or unbelief.

It is more than possible that God is even now imparting the gifts of the Spirit to whomsoever He can and in whatever measure He can as His conditions are met even imperfectly. Otherwise the torch of truth would flicker out and die.

Clearly, however, we have yet to see what God would do for His Church if we would all throw ourselves down before Him with an open Bible and cry, "Behold Thy servant, Lord! Be it unto me even as Thou wilt."

How To Be Filled With The Spirit

Almost all Christians want to be full of the Spirit. Only a few want to be filled with the Spirit.

But how can a Christian know the fullness of the Spirit unless he has known the experience of being filled?

It would, however, be useless to tell anyone how to be filled with the Spirit unless he first believes that he can be. No one can hope for something he is not convinced is the will of God for him and within the bounds of scriptural provision.

Before the question "How can I be filled?" has any validity the seeker after God must be sure that the experience of being filled is actually possible. The man who is not sure can have no ground of expectation. Where there is no expectation there can be no faith, and where there is no faith the inquiry is meaningless.

The doctrine of the Spirit as it relates to the believer has over the last half century been shrouded in a mist such as lies upon a mountain in stormy weather. A world of confusion has surrounded this truth. The children of God have been taught contrary doctrines from the same texts, warned, threatened and intimidated until they instinctively recoil from every mention of the Bible teaching concerning the Holy Spirit.

This confusion has not come by accident. An enemy has done this. Satan knows that Spiritless evangelicalism is as deadly as Modernism or heresy, and he has done everything in his power to prevent us from enjoying our true Christian heritage.

A church without the Spirit is as helpless as Israel might have been in the wilderness if the fiery cloud had deserted them. The Holy Spirit is our cloud by day and our fire by night. Without Him we only wander aimlessly about the dessert.

That is what we today are surely doing. We have divided ourselves into little ragged groups, each one running after a will-o'-the-wisp or firefly in the mistaken notion that we are following the Shekinah. It is not only desirable that the cloudy pillar should begin to glow again. It is imperative.

The Church can have light only as it is full of the Spirit, and it can be full only as the members that compose it are filled individually. Furthermore, no one can be filled until he is convinced that being filled is a part of the total plan of God in redemption; that it is nothing added or extra, nothing strange or queer, but a proper and spiritual operation of God, based upon and growing out of the work of Christ in atonement.

The inquirer must be sure to the point of conviction. He must believe that the whole thing is normal and right. He must believe that God wills that he be anointed with a horn of fresh oil beyond and in addition to all the ten thousand blessings he may already have received from the good hand of God.

Until he is so convinced I recommend that he take time out to fast and pray and meditate upon the Scriptures. Faith comes from the Word of God. Suggestion, exhortation or the psychological effect of the testimony of others who may have been filled will not suffice.

Unless he is persuaded from the Scriptures, he should not press the matter nor allow himself to fall victim to the emotional manipulators intent upon forcing the issue. God is wonderfully patient and understanding and will wait for the slow heart to catch up with the truth. In the meantime, the seeker should be calm and confident. In due time God will lead him through the Jordan. Let him not break loose and run ahead. Too many have done so, only to bring disaster upon their Christian lives.

After a man is convinced that he can be filled with the Spirit he must desire to be. To the interested inquirer I ask these questions: Are you sure that you want to be possessed by a Spirit Who, while He is pure and gentle and wise and loving, will yet insist upon being Lord of your life? Are you sure you want your personality to be taken over by One Who will require obedience to the written Word? Who will not tolerate any of the self-sins in your life: self-love, self-indulgence? Who will not permit you to strut or boast or show off? Who will take the direction of your life away from you and will reserve the sovereign right to test you and discipline you? Who will strip away from you many loved objects which secretly harm your soul?

Unless you can answer an eager "Yes" to these questions you do not want to be filled. You may want the thrill or the victory or the power, but you do not really want to be filled with the Spirit. Your desire is little more than a feeble wish and is not pure enough to please God, Who demands all or nothing.

Again I ask: Are you sure you need to be filled with the Spirit? Tens of thousands of Christians, laymen, preachers, missionaries, manage to get on somehow without having had a clear experience of being filled. That Spiritless labor can lead only to tragedy in the day of Christ is something the average Christian seems to have forgotten. But how about you?

Perhaps your doctrinal bias is away from belief in the crisis of the Spirit's filling. Very well, look at the fruit of such doctrine. What is your life producing? You are doing religious work, preaching, singing, writing, promoting, but what is the quality of your work? True; you received the Spirit at the moment of conversion, but is it also true that you are ready without a further anointing to resist temptation, obey the Scriptures, understand the truth, live victoriously, die in peace and meet Christ without embarrassment at His coming?

If, on the other hand, your soul cries out for God, for the living God, and your dry and empty heart despairs of living a normal Christian life without a further anointing, then I ask you: Is your desire all-absorbing? Is it the biggest thing in your life? Does it crowd out every common religious activity and fill you with an acute longing that can only be described as the pain of desire? If your heart cries "Yes" to these questions you may be on your way to a spiritual breakthrough that will transform your whole life.

It is in the preparation for receiving the Spirit's anointing that most Christians fail. Probably no one was ever filled without first having gone through a period of deep soul disturbance and inward turmoil. When we find ourselves entering this state the temptation is to panic and draw back. Satan exhorts us to take it easy lest we make shipwreck of the faith, and dishonor the Lord that bought us.

Of course, he cares nothing for us nor for our Lord. His purpose is to keep us weak and unarmed in a day of conflict. And millions of believers accept his hypocritical lies as gospel truth and go back to their caves like the prophets of Obadiah to feed on bread and water.

Before there can be fullness there must be emptiness. Before God can fill us with Himself, we must first be emptied of ourselves. It is this emptying that brings the painful disappointment and despair of self of which so many persons have complained just prior to their new and radiant experience.

There must come a total of self-disvaluation, a death to all things without us and within us, or there can never be a real filling with the Holy Spirit.

The dearest idol I have known,
Whate'er that idol be,
Help me to tear it from Thy throne,
And worship only Thee.

We sing this glibly enough, but we cancel out our prayer by our refusal to surrender the very idol of which we sing. To give up our last idol is to plunge ourselves into a state of inward loneliness which no gospel meeting, no fellowship with other Christians, can ever cure. For this reason, most Christians play it safe and settle for a life of compromise.

They have some of God, to be sure, but not all; and God has some of them, but not all. And so, they live their tepid lives and try to disguise with bright smiles and snappy choruses the deep spiritual destitution within them.

One thing should be made crystal clear: The soul's journey through the dark night is not a meritorious one. The suffering and the loneliness do not make a man dear to God nor earn the horn of oil for which he yearns. We cannot buy anything from God. Everything comes out of His goodness on the grounds of Christ's redeeming blood and is a free gift, with no strings attached.

What the soul agony does is to break up the fallow ground, empty the vessel, detach the heart from earthly interests and focus the attention upon God.

All that has gone before is by way of soul preparation for the divine act of infilling. The infilling itself is not a complicated thing. While I shy away from "how to" formulas in spiritual things, I believe the answer to the question "How can I be filled?" may be answered in four words, all of them active verbs. They are these: (1) surrender, (2) ask, (3) obey, (4) believe.

Surrender: "I beseech you therefore, brethren, by the mercies of God, that ye present your bodies a living sacrifice, holy, acceptable unto God, which is your reasonable service. And be not conformed to this world: but be ye transformed by the renewing of your mind, that ye may prove what is that good, and acceptable, and perfect, will of God" (Rom. 12:1,2).

Ask: "If ye then, being evil, know how to give good gifts unto your children: how much more shall your heavenly Father give the Holy Spirit to them that ask him?" (Luke 11:13).

Obey: "We are his witnesses of these things; and so is also the Holy Ghost, whom God hath given to them that obey him" (Acts 5:32).

Complete and ungrudging obedience to the will of God is absolutely indispensable to the reception of the Spirit's anointing. As we wait before God we should reverently search the Scriptures and listen for the voice of gentle stillness to learn what our Heavenly Father expects of us. Then, trusting to His enabling, we should obey to the best of our ability and understanding.

Believe: This only would I learn of you, Received ye the Spirit by the works of the law, or by the hearing of faith?" (Gal. 3:2).

While the infilling of the Spirit is received by faith and only by faith, let us beware of that imitation faith which is no more than a mental assent to truth. It has been a source of great disappointment to multitudes of seeking souls. True faith invariably brings a witness.

But what is that witness? It is nothing physical, vocal nor psychical. The Spirit never commits Himself to the flesh. The only witness He gives is a subjective one, known to the individual alone. The Spirit announces Himself to the deep-in spirit of the man. The flesh profiteth nothing, but the believing heart knows. Holy, holy, holy.

One last thing: Neither in the Old Testament nor in the New, nor in Christian testimony as found in the writings of the saints as far as my knowledge goes, was any believer ever filled with the Holy Spirit who did not know he had been filled. Neither was anyone filled who did not know when he was filled. And no one was ever filled gradually.

Behind these three trees many half-hearted souls have tried to hide like Adam from the presence of the Lord, but they are not good enough hiding places. The man who does not know when he was filled was never filled (though of course it is possible to forget the date). And the man who hopes to be filled gradually will never be filled at all.

In my sober judgment the relation of the Spirit to the believer is the most vital question the church faces today. The problems raised by Christian existentialism or neo-orthodoxy are nothing by comparison with this most critical one. Ecumenicity, eschatological theories—none of these things deserve consideration until every believer can give an affirmative answer to the question, "Have ye received the Holy Ghost since ye believed?"

And it might easily be that after we have been filled with the Spirit we will find to our delight that the very filling itself has solved the other problems for us.

How to be Filled with the Holy Spirit

[1960]

Preface

The following pages represent the gist of a series of sermons given on successive Sunday evenings to the congregation of the church of which I am pastor. The talks were taken down stenographically and later reduced to their present length. A fifth message which was a part of the series has been omitted here.

The fact that these were originally spoken messages accounts for their racy style and for the personal references which occur in them occasionally. Had I been writing the messages I should have exercised greater care in the composition. The subject is, however, so vitally important that I feel sure the reader will pardon the offhand style of the language. The truth is always good even when the vehicle in which it rides is homely and plain.

This booklet is made available to the Christian public with the prayer that it may help to lead many thirsty believers to the fountain of living waters.

—*A. W. T.*

Who is the Holy Spirit?

We all use the word "spirit" a great deal. Now I want to tell you what I do and do not mean by it. In the first place, we rule out all of the secondary uses of the word "spirit." I do not mean courage, as when we say, "That's the spirit!" I don't mean temper or temperament or pluck. I mean nothing so nebulous as that. Spirit is a specific and identifiable substance. If not definable, it can at least be described. Spirit is as real as matter, but it is another mode of being than matter.

We are all materialists to some extent. We are born of material parents into a material world; we are wrapped in material clothes and fed on material milk and lie in a material bed, and sleep and walk and live and talk and grow up in a world of matter. Matter presses upon us obtrusively and takes over our thinking so completely that we cannot speak of spirit without using materialistic terms. God made man out of the dust of the ground, and man has been dust ever since, and we can't quite shake it off.

Matter is one mode of being; spirit is another mode of being as authentic as matter.

Material things have certain characteristics. For instance, they have weight. Everything that is material weighs something; it yields to gravitational pull. Then, matter has dimensions; you can measure the thing if it is made of matter. It has shape. It has an outline of some sort, no matter whether it is a molecule or an atom or whatever it may be, on up to the stars that shine. Then, it is extended in space. So I say that weight, dimension, shape and extension are the things that belong to matter. That is one mode of being; that is one way of existing.

One power of spirit, of any spirit (for I am talking about spirit now, not about the Holy Spirit), is its ability to penetrate. Matter bumps against other matter and stops; it cannot penetrate. Spirit can penetrate everything. For instance, your body is made of matter, and yet your spirit has penetrated your body completely. Spirit can penetrate spirit. It can penetrate personality—oh, if God's people could only learn that spirit can penetrate personality, that your personality is not an impenetrable substance, but can be penetrated. A mind can be penetrated by thought, and the air can be penetrated by light, and material things and mental things, and even spiritual things, can be penetrated by spirit.

Now, what is the Holy Spirit? Not who, but what? The answer is that the Holy Spirit is a Being dwelling in another mode of existence. He has not weight, nor measure, nor size, nor any color, no extension in space, but He nevertheless exists as surely as you exist.

The Holy Spirit is not enthusiasm. I have found enthusiasm that hummed with excitement, and the Holy Spirit was nowhere to be found there at all; and I have found the Holy Ghost when there has not been much of what we call enthusiasm present. Neither is the Holy Spirit another name for genius. We talk about the spirit of Beethoven and say, "This or that artist played with great spirit. He interpreted the spirit of the master." The Holy Spirit is none of these things. Now what is He?

He is a Person. Put that down in capital letters—that the Holy Spirit is not only a Being having another mode of existence, but He is Himself a Person, with all the qualities and powers of personality. He is not matter, but He is substance. The Holy Spirit is often thought of as a beneficent wind that blows across the Church. If you think of the Holy Spirit as being literally a wind, a breath, then you think of Him as nonpersonal and nonindividual. But the Holy Spirit has will and intelligence and feeling and knowledge and sympathy and ability to love and see and flunk and hear and speak and desire the same as any person has.

You may say, "I believe all that. You surely don't think you are telling us anything new!" I don't hope to tell you very much that is new; I only hope to set the table for you, arranging the dishes a little better and a little more attractively so that you will be tempted to partake. Many of us have grown up on the theology that accepts the Holy Spirit as a Person, and even as a divine Person, but for some reason it never did us any good. We are as empty as ever, we are as joyless as ever, we are as far from peace as ever, we are as weak as ever. What I want to do is to tell you the old things, but while I am doing it, to encourage your heart to make them yours now, and to walk into the living, throbbing, vibrating heart of them, so that from here on your life will be altogether different.

So the Spirit is a Person. That's what He is. Now, who is He?

The historic church has said that He is God. Let me quote from the Nicene Creed: "I believe in the Holy Ghost, the Lord and Giver of life, Which proceedeth from the Father and the Son, and with the Father and the Son together is worshipped and glorified."

That is what the Church believed about the Holy Ghost 1,600 years ago. Let's be daring for a moment. Let's try to think away this idea that the Holy Spirit is truly God. All right. Let's admit something else into the picture. Let's say, "I believe in one Holy Ghost, the Lord and Giver of life, who with the Father and the Son is to be worshiped and glorified." For the "Holy Ghost" let's put in "Abraham, the father of the faithful, who with the Father and the Son together is worshiped and glorified." That is a monstrous thing, and in your heart already there is a shocked feeling. You couldn't do it. You couldn't admit a mere man into the holy circle of the Trinity! The Father and the Son are to be worshiped and glorified, and if the Holy Spirit is to be included here. He has to be equal to the Father and the Son.

Now let's look at the Athanasian Creed. Thirteen hundred years old it is. Notice what it says about the Holy Spirit: "Such as the Father is, such is the Son, and such is the Holy Ghost." Once more let's do that terrible thing. Let's introduce into this concept the name of a man. Let's put David in there. Let's say, "Such as the Father is, such also is the Son, and such is the hymnist David." That would be a shock like cold water in the face! You can't do that. And you can't put the archangel Michael in there. You can't say, "Such as the Father is, such also is the Son, and such is the archangel Michael." That would be a monstrous inconsistency, and you know it!

I have told you what the great creeds of the church say. If the Bible taught otherwise, I would throw the creeds away. Nobody can come down the years with flowing beard, and with the dust of centuries upon him, and get me to believe a doctrine unless he can give me chapter and verse. I quote the creeds, but I preach them only so far as they summarize the teaching of the Bible on a given subject. If there were divergency from the teachings of the Word of God I would not teach the creed; I would teach the Book, for the Book is the source of all authentic information. However, our fathers did a mighty good job of going into the Bible, finding out what it taught, and then formulating the creeds for us.

Now let's look at what our song writers and our hymnists believed. Recall the words the quartet sang this evening:

> "Holy Ghost, with light divine,
> Shine upon this heart of mine."

Let's pray that prayer to Gabriel, to Saint Bernard, to D. L. Moody. Let's pray that prayer to any man or any creature that has ever served God. You can't pray that kind of prayer to a creature. To put those words into a hymn means that the one about whom you are speaking must be God.

> *"Holy Ghost, with power divine,*
> *Cleanse this guilty heart of mine."*

Who can get into the intricate depths of a human soul, into the deep confines of a human spirit and cleanse it? Nobody but the God who made it! The hymn writer who said "Cleanse this guilty heart of mine" meant that the Holy Ghost to whom he prayed was God.

> *"Holy Spirit, all divine,*
> *Dwell within this heart of mine;*
> *Cast down every idol throne,*
> *Reign supreme—and reign alone."*

The church has sung that now for about one hundred years. "Reign supreme—and reign alone." Could you pray that to anybody you know? The man who wrote that hymn believed that the Holy Ghost was God, otherwise he wouldn't have said, "Reign supreme, and reign all by Yourself." That is an invitation no man can make to anybody, except the Divine One, except God.

Now the Scriptures. Notice that I am trying to establish the truth that the Holy Spirit is not only a Person, but that He is a divine Person; not only a divine Person, but God.

In Psalm 139 the hymnist attributes omnipresence to the Holy Ghost. He says, "Whither shall I go from thy spirit? or whither shall I flee from thy presence?" and he develops throughout the 139th Psalm, in language that is as beautiful as a sunrise and as musical as the wind through the willows, the idea that the Spirit is everywhere, having the attributes of deity. He must be deity, for no creature could have the attributes of deity.

In Hebrews (9: 14) there is attributed to the Holy Ghost that which is never attributed to an archangel, or a seraphim, or a cherubim, or an angel, or an apostle, or a martyr, or a prophet, or a patriarch, or anyone that has ever been created by the hand of God. It says, "Through the eternal Spirit," and every theologian knows that eternity is an attribute of no creature which deity has ever formed. The angels are not eternal; that is, they had a beginning, and all created things had beginning. As soon as the word "eternal" is used about a being it immediately establishes the fact that he never had a beginning, is not a creature at all, but God. Therefore, when the Holy Ghost says "the eternal Spirit" about Himself He is calling Himself God.

Again, the baptismal formula in Matthew 28 says, "Baptizing them in the name of the Father, and of the Son, and of the Holy Ghost." Now try to imagine putting the name of a man in there. "Baptizing them in the name of the Father and the Son and the Apostle Paul." You couldn't think it! It is horrible to contemplate! No man can be admitted into that closed circle of deity. We baptize in the name of the Father and the Son, because the Son is equal with the Father in His Godhead, and we baptize in the name of the Holy Ghost because the Holy Ghost is also equal with the Father and the Son.

You say, "You are just a Trinitarian and we are Trinitarians already." Yes, I know it, but once again I tell you that I am trying to throw emphasis upon this teaching.

How many blessed truths have gotten snowed under. People believe them, but they are just not being taught, that is all. I think of our experience this morning. Here was a man and his wife, a very fine intelligent couple from another city. They named the church to which they belonged, and I instantly said, "That is a fine church!" "Oh, yes," they said, "but they don't teach what we came over here for." They came over because they were ill and wanted to be scripturally anointed for healing. So I got together two missionaries, two preachers, and an elder, and we anointed them and prayed for them. If you were to go to that church where they attend and say to the preacher, "Do you believe that the Lord answers prayer and heals the sick?" he would reply, "Sure, I do!" He believes it, but he doesn't teach it, and what you don't believe strongly enough to teach doesn't do you any good.

It is the same with the fullness of the Holy Ghost. Evangelical Christianity believes it, but nobody experiences it. It lies under the snow, forgotten. I am praying that God may be able to melt away the ice from this blessed truth, and let it spring up again alive, that the Church and the people who hear may get some good out of it and not merely say "I believe" while it is buried under the snow of inactivity and nonattention.

Let us recapitulate. Who is the Spirit? The Spirit is God, existing in another mode of being than ourselves. He exists as a spirit and not as matter, for He is not matter, but He is God. He is a Person. It was so believed by the whole Church of Christ down through the years. It was so sung by the hymnists back in the days of the first hymn writers. It is so taught in the Book, all through the Old Testament and the New, and I have given you only a few proof texts. I could spend the evening reading Scripture stating this same thing.

Now what follows from all this? Ah, there is an unseen Deity present, a knowing, feeling Personality, and He is indivisible from the Father and the Son, so that if you were to be suddenly transferred to heaven itself you wouldn't be any closer to God than you are now, for God is already here. Changing your geographical location would not bring you any nearer to God nor God any nearer to you, because the indivisible Trinity is present, and all that the Son is the Holy Ghost is, and all that the Father is the Holy Ghost is, and the Holy Ghost is in His Church.

What will we find Him to be like? He will be exactly like Jesus. You have read your New Testament, and you know what Jesus is like, and the Holy Spirit is exactly like Jesus, for Jesus was God and the Spirit is God, and the Father is exactly like the Son; and you can know what Jesus is like by knowing what the Father is like, and you can know what the Spirit is like by knowing what Jesus is like.

If Jesus were to come walking down this aisle there would be no stampede for the door. Nobody would scream and be frightened. We might begin to weep for sheer joy and delight that He had so honored us, but nobody would be afraid of Jesus; no mother with a little crying babe would ever have to be afraid of Jesus; no poor harlot being dragged by the hair of her head had to be afraid of Jesus—nobody! Nobody ever need to be afraid of Jesus, because He is the epitome of love, kindliness, geniality, warm attractiveness and sweetness. And that is exactly what the Holy Ghost is, for He is the Spirit of the Father and the Son. Amen.

THE PROMISE OF THE FATHER

"And, behold, I send the promise of my Father upon you: but tarry ye in the city of Jerusalem, until ye be endued with power from on high" Luke 24: 49.

I wonder if you have ever thought of the origin of the phrase Jesus used here. Why did He call it the Father's promise? He didn't say "mine." He said, "The promise of my Father." This takes us back to Joel 2: 28, 29.

"And it shall come to pass afterward, that I will pour out my spirit upon all flesh; and your sons and your daughters shall prophesy, your old men shall dream dreams, your young men shall see visions: and also upon the servants and upon the handmaids in those days will I pour out my spirit."

Now, when our Lord Jesus came He authoritatively interpreted this, and tied up His intention for His Church with the ancient promises given by the Father centuries before.

In fulfillment of all this there were three periods discernible in the New Testament: (1) The period of the promise; (2) the period of the preparation, and (3) the period of the realization-all this having to do with the promise of the Father and the intention of the Son toward His people.

The period of the promise extends from John the Baptist, roughly, to the resurrection of our Lord Jesus. The marks of it are these: that there were disciples, and they were commissioned and instructed, and they exercised their commission and the authority granted them by the Lord. They knew the Lord Jesus; they loved Him. They knew Him living, they knew Him and saw Him dead, and they saw Him risen again from the dead. All the time our Lord was with them He was busy creating expectation in them. He was telling His disciples that in spite of all they had and all the blessing that God the Father had given them, they were still to expect the coming of a new and superior kind of life. He was creating an expectation of an effusion of outpoured energy which they, at their best, did not yet enjoy.

Then our Lord rose from the dead and we have what we call the period of the preparation. That was the short period which intervened between our Lord's resurrection and the down coming of the Holy Ghost. They had stopped their activity at the specific command of the Lord. He said, "Tarry! You are about to receive that which has been promised. Your expectations are about to be fulfilled; your hopes realized. Therefore, don't do anything until it comes."

I might say here that sometimes you are going farther when you are not going anywhere; you are moving faster when you are not moving at all; you are learning more when you think you have stopped learning. These disciples had reached an impasse. Their Lord had risen, and they had seen Him, and with excitement and joy they knew He had risen from the dead. Now He had gone from them. Where was He? They gathered together, as you and I might have done under like circumstances, waiting, all of one accord. That is more than they had done during the period of the promise. But here were 120 of them, and they had a oneness of accord.

The period of realization came upon them when the Father fulfilled His promise and sent the Spirit. Peter used a phrase to describe it which is one of the fullest, finest phrases I know. He said, "He hath shed forth this, which ye now see and hear"— the shedding forth was like a mighty down coming of water. The expectations were more than met—not fully met, but more than met. God always gives us an overplus. They got more than they expected.

Now what happened here? What did they receive that they had not had before? Well, first, they had a new kind of evidence for the reality of their faith. You see, Christ talked about four lines of evidence of His Messiahship.

He said: "Search the scriptures; for in them ye think ye have eternal life: and they are they which testify of me." The Scriptures were proof of who Christ was. That is one line of evidence.

Another line is the witness of John the Baptist who pointed to Jesus and said, "Behold, the Lamb of God, that taketh away the sin of the world!"

Jesus gives us another line of evidence. He said, "The Father himself . . . hath borne witness of me," and there was the third proof of His Messiahship, an authentic proof of it.

He gave a fourth. He said, "The same works that I do, bear witness of me, that the Father hath sent me." "Believe me for the very works' sake." Have you noticed there is one serious breakdown there, a breakdown which our Lord recognized and which He remedied when the Holy Spirit came? That breakdown lies in the necessary externality of the proof. In every instance the proofs which our Lord adduced to His own Messiahship were external to the individual. They are not inside of the man. He has to open the Book and read. That is external to the man.

When I hear that the Church of Christ has gone throughout the whole world carrying the torch of civilization, healing and giving hope and help, I conclude the Christian Church must be of God because she is acting the way God would act. When I hear that she has founded hospitals and insane asylums, I say surely she must be of God because that is what God would do, being what He is. When I hear that she has emancipated woman and has taken her from being a chattel slave and an object of some old king's lust to being the equal of the man and queen in his home, I say surely that must be of God. You can go down the corridors of history, and you can adduce proof of the divinity of the Church from what the Church has done. You can show how she brought civilization here and she brought help there. She cleaned up saloons in this town, and she delivered this young fellow from drink. We say that must be God. But that is external proof and it depends upon logic.

There is another kind of evidence. It is the immediate evidence of the inner life. That is the evidence by which you know you are alive. If I were to prove that you weren't alive, you would chuckle and go home just as alive as you are now and not a bit worried about it, because you have the instant, unmediated evidence of internal life.

Jesus Christ wanted to take religion out of the external and make it internal and put it on the same level as life itself, so that a man knows he knows God the same as he knows he is himself and not somebody else. He knows he knows God the same as he knows he is alive and not dead. Only the Holy Ghost can do that. The Holy Spirit came to carry the evidence of Christianity from the books of apologetics into the human heart, and that is exactly what He does. You can take the gospel of Jesus Christ to the heathen in Borneo, or Africa, people who could never conceive the first premise of your logical arguments, so that it would be totally impossible for them to decide on logical grounds whether Christianity was of God or not. Preach Christ to them and they will believe and be transformed and put away their wickedness and change from evil to righteousness and get happy about it all, learn to read and write and study their Bibles and become leaders and pillars in their church, transformed and made over. How? By the instant witness of the Holy Ghost to their hearts. This is the new thing that came, sir! God took religion from the realm of the external and made it internal.

Our trouble is that we are trying to confirm the truth of Christianity by an appeal to external evidence. We are saying, "Well, look at this fellow. He can throw a baseball farther than anybody else and he is a Christian, therefore Christianity must be true." "Here is a great statesman who believes the Bible. Therefore, the Bible must be true." We quote Daniel Webster, or Roger Bacon. We write books to show that some scientist believed in Christianity: therefore, Christianity must be true. We are all the way out on the wrong track, brother! That is not New Testament Christianity at all. That is a pitiful, whimpering, drooling appeal to the flesh. That never was the testimony of the New Testament, never the way God did things—never! You might satisfy the intellects of men by external evidences, and Christ did, I say, point to external evidence when He was here on the earth. But He said, "I am sending you something better. I am taking Christian apologetics out of the realm of logic and putting it into the realm of life. I am proving My deity, and My proof will not be an appeal to a general or a prime minister. The proof lies in an invisible, unseen but powerful energy that visits the human soul when the gospel is preached—the Holy Ghost!" The Spirit of the living God brought an evidence that needed no logic; it went straight to the soul like a flash of silver light, like the direct plunge of a sharp spear into the heart. Those are the very words that the Scriptures use when it says "pierced (pricked) to the heart." One translator points out that that word "pricked" is a word that means that it goes in deeper than the spear that pierced Jesus' side!

That is the way God does. There is an immediate witness, an unmediated push of the Spirit of God upon the spirit of man. There is a filtering down, a getting down into the very cells of the human soul and the impression on that soul by the Holy Ghost that this is true. That is what those disciples had never had before, and that is exactly what the Church does not have now. That is what we fundamentalist preachers wish we had and don't have, and that is why we are going so far astray to prove things. That, incidentally, is why this humble pulpit is never open to a man who wants to prove Christianity by means of appeal to external evidence. You can't do it to begin with, and I wouldn't do it to end with. We have something better.

Then, also, the Spirit gave a bright, emotional quality to their religion, and I grieve before my God over the lack of this in our day. The emotional quality isn't there. There is a sickliness about us all; we pump so hard trying to get a little drop of delight out of our old rusty well, and we write innumerable bouncy choruses, and we pump and pump until you can hear the old rusty thing squeak across forty acres. But it doesn't work.

Then He gave them direct spiritual authority. By that I mean He removed their fears, their questions, their apologies, and their doubts, and they had an authority that was founded upon life.

There is a great modern error which I want to mention: it is that the coming of the Spirit happened once for all, that the individual Christian is not affected by it. It is like the birth of Christ which happened once for all and the most excellent sermon on the birth of Christ would never have that birth repeated, and all the prayers in the wide world would never have Christ born again of the Virgin Mary. It is, they say, like the death and resurrection of Christ—never to be repeated. This error asserts that the coming of the Holy Spirit is an historic thing, an advance in the dispensational workings of God; but that it is all settled now and we need give no further thought to it. It is all here and we have it all, and if we believe in Christ that is it and there isn't anything more.

All right. Now everybody has a right to his or her view, if he thinks it is scriptural; but I would just like to ask some questions. I won't answer them; I'll just ask them, and you preach your own sermon.

Is the promise of the Father, with all its attendant riches of spiritual grace and power, intended to be for first-century Christians only? Does the new birth, which the first-century Christians had to have, suffice for all other Christians, or is the new birth which they had to have that which we have to have? Does the new birth have to be repeated in each Christian before it is valid, or did that first church get born again for us? Can you get born again by proxy? The fact that those first 120 were born again, does that mean that we don't have to be? Now you answer me.

You say, "No, certainly we agree that everybody has to have the new birth for himself, individually." All right, if that is true (and it is), is the fullness of the Spirit which those first Christians received enough? Does that work for you and me? They had the fullness; now they are dead. Does the fact that they were filled avail for me? You answer that question.

Again, I want to ask you, would a meal eaten by Saint Peter in the year 33 A. D. nourish me today? Would a good meal of barley cakes and milk, and honey spread on the barley cake— a good meal for a good Jew in Peter's day—nourish me today? No, Peter is dead, and I can't be nourished by what Peter ate.

Would the fullness of the Holy Ghost that Peter got in the upper chamber do for me today, or must I receive individually what Peter received?

What value would the fullness of the Spirit in the church in Jerusalem have for us today if it was done over there once for all and we can't have the same thing here? We are separated by 5,000 miles of water and by 1,900 years of time. Now what, that happened to them, can possibly avail for us?

I want to ask you some more questions: Do you see any similarity between the average one of us Christians buzzing around Chicago and those apostles? Are you ready to believe that we have just what they had, and that every believer in Chicago who accepts the Bible and is converted immediately enters into and now enjoys and possesses exactly what they did back there? Surely you know better than that!

This modern fundamentalism as we know it and of which we are a part—is it a satisfactory fulfillment of the expectations raised by the Father and Christ? Our Father who is in heaven raised certain high expectations of what He was going to do for His redeemed people. When His Son came to redeem those people, He heightened those expectations, raised them, clarified them, extended them, enlarged them, and emphasized them. He raised an expectation that was simply beyond words, too wonderful and beautiful and thrilling to imagine. I want to ask you: Is this level of Christianity which we fundamentalists in this city now enjoy what He meant by what He said?

Listen, brother. Our Lord Jesus Christ advertised that He was going away to the Father and He was going to send back for His people a wonderful gift, and He said, "Stay right here until it comes, because it will be the difference between failure and success to you."

Then the Spirit came. Was He equal to the advertising? Did they say, "Is this all He meant! Oh, it is disappointing!" No. The Scripture says they wondered. The word "wonder" is in their mouths and hearts. He gave so much more than He promised, because words were the promise and the Holy Ghost was the fulfillment.

The simple fact is that we believers are not up to what He gave us reason to expect. The only honest thing to do is admit this and do something about it. There certainly has been a vast breakdown somewhere between promise and fulfillment. That breakdown is not with our heavenly Father, for He always gives more than He promises.

Now I am going to ask that you reverently ponder this and set aside time and search the Scriptures, pray and yield, obey and believe, and see whether that which our Lord gave us reason to think could be the possession of the Church may not be ours in actual fulfillment and realization.

How to be Filled, with the Holy Spirit

Before we deal with the question of how to be filled with the Holy Spirit, there are some matters which first have to be settled. As believers you have to get them out of the way, and right here is where the difficulty arises. I have been afraid that my listeners might have gotten the idea somewhere that I had a how-to-be-filled-with-the-Spirit-in-five-easy-lessons doctrine, which I could give you. If you have any such vague ideas as that, I can only stand before you and say, "I am sorry"; because it isn't true; I can't give you such a course. There are some things, I say, that you have to get out of the way, settled. One of them is: Before you are filled with the Holy Spirit you must be sure that you can be filled.

Satan has opposed the doctrine of the Spirit-filled life about as bitterly as any other doctrine there is. He has confused it, opposed it, surrounded it with false notions and fears. He has blocked every effort of the Church of Christ to receive from the Father her divine and blood-bought patrimony. The Church has tragically neglected this great liberating truth—that there is now for the child of God a full and wonderful and completely satisfying anointing with the Holy Ghost.

So you have to be sure that it is for you. You must be sure that it is God's will for you; that is, that it is part of the total plan, that it is included and embraced within the work of Christ in redemption; that it is, as the old camp-meeting, praying folks used to say, "the purchase of His blood."

I might throw a bracket in here and say that whenever I use the neutral pronoun "it" I am talking about the gift. When I speak directly of the Holy Spirit, I shall use a personal pronoun, He or Him or His, referring to a person, for the Holy Spirit is not an it, but the gift of the Holy Spirit must necessarily in our English language be called "it."

You must, I say, be satisfied that this is nothing added or extra. The Spirit-filled life is not a special, deluxe edition of Christianity. It is part and parcel of the total plan of God for His people.

You must be satisfied that it is not abnormal. I admit that it is unusual, because there are so few people who walk in the light of it or enjoy it, but it is not abnormal. In a world where everybody was sick, health would be unusual, but it wouldn't be abnormal. This is unusual only because our spiritual lives are so wretchedly sick and so far down from where they should be.

You must be satisfied, again, that there is nothing about the Holy Spirit queer or strange or eerie. I believe it has been the work of the devil to surround the person of the Holy Spirit with an aura of queerness, or strangeness, so that the people of God feel that this Spirit-filled life is a life of being odd and peculiar, of being a bit uncanny.

That is not true, my friend! The devil manufactured that. He hatched it out, the same devil that once said to our ancient mother, "Yea, hath God said," and thus maligned God Almighty. That same devil has maligned the Holy Ghost. There is nothing eerie, nothing queer, nothing contrary to the normal operations of the human heart about the Holy Ghost. He is only the essence of Jesus imparted to believers. You read the four Gospels and see for yourself how wonderfully calm, pure, sane, simple, sweet, natural, and lovable Jesus was. Even philosophers who don't believe in His deity have to admit the lovableness of His character.

You must be sure of all this to the point of conviction. That is, you must be convinced to a point where you won't try to persuade God.

You don't have to persuade God at all. There is no persuasion necessary. Dr. Simpson used to say, "Being filled with the Spirit is as easy as breathing; you can simply breathe out and breathe in." He wrote a hymn to that effect. I am sorry that it is not a better hymn, because it is wonderful theology.

Unless you have arrived at this place in your listening and thinking and meditating and praying, where you know that the Spirit-filled life is for you, that there is no doubt about it—no book you read or sermon you heard, or tract somebody sent you is bothering you; you are restful about all this; you are convinced that in the blood of Jesus when He died on the cross there was included, as a purchase of that blood, your right to a full, Spirit-filled life—unless you are convinced of that, unless you are convinced that it isn't an added, unusual, extra, deluxe something that you have to go to God and beg and beat your fists on the chair to get, I recommend this to you: I recommend that you don't do anything about it yet except to meditate upon the Scriptures bearing on this truth. Go to the Word of God and to those parts of it which deal with the subject under discussion tonight and meditate upon them; for "faith cometh by hearing, and hearing by the word of God." Real faith springs not out of sermons but out of the

Word of God and out of sermons only so far as they are of the Word of God. I recommend that you be calm and confident about this. Don't get excited, don't despond. The darkest hour is just before the dawn. It may be that this moment of discouragement which you are going through is preliminary to a sunburst of new and beautiful living, if you will follow on to know the Lord.

Remember, fear is of the flesh and panic is of the devil. Never fear and never get panicky. When they came to Jesus nobody except a hypocrite ever needed to fear Him. When a hypocrite came to Jesus He just sliced him to bits and sent him away bleeding from every pore. If they were ready to give up their sin and follow the Lord and they came in simplicity of heart and said, "Lord, what do You want me to do?" the Lord took all the time in the world to talk to them and explain to them and to correct any false impressions or wrong ideas they had. He is the sweetest, most understanding and wonderful Teacher in the world, and He never panics anybody. It is sin that does that. If there is a sense of panic upon your life, it may be because there is sin in that life of yours which you need to get rid of.

Again, before you can be filled with the Spirit you must desire to be filled. Here I meet with a certain amount of puzzlement. Somebody will say, "How is it that you say to us that we must desire to be filled, because you know we desire to be. Haven't we talked to you in person? Haven't we called you on the phone? Aren't we out here tonight to hear the sermon on the Holy Spirit? Isn't this all a comforting indication to you that we are desirous of being filled with the Holy Spirit?"

Not necessarily, and I will explain why. For instance, are you sure that you want to be possessed by a spirit other than your own? Even though that spirit be the pure Spirit of God? even though He be the very gentle essence of the gentle Jesus? even though He be sane and pure and free? even though He be wisdom personified, wisdom Himself, even though He have a healing, precious ointment to distill? even though He be loving as the heart of God? That Spirit, if He ever possesses you, will be the Lord of your Life!

I ask you, Do you want Him to be Lord of your life? That you want His benefits, I know. I take that for granted. But do you want to be possessed by Him? Do you want to hand the keys of your soul over to the Holy Spirit and say, "Lord, from now on I don't even have a key to my own house. I come and go as Thou tellest me"? Are you willing to give the office of your business establishment, your soul, over to the Lord and say to Jesus, "You sit in this chair and handle these telephones and boss the staff and be Lord of this outfit"? That is what 1 mean. Are you sure you want this? Are you sure that you desire it?

Are you sure that you want your personality to be taken over by One who will expect obedience to the written and living Word? Are you sure that you want your personality to be taken over by One who will not tolerate the self sins? For instance, self-love. You can no more have the Holy Ghost and have self-love than you can have purity and impurity at the same moment in the same place. He will not permit you to indulge self-confidence. Self-love, self-confidence, self-righteousness, self-admiration, self-aggrandizement, and self-pity are under the interdiction of God Almighty, and He cannot send His mighty Spirit to possess the heart where these things are.

Again, I ask you if you desire to have your personality taken over by One who stands in sharp opposition to the world's easy ways? No tolerance of evil, no smiling at crooked jokes, no laughing off things that God hates. The Spirit of God, if He takes over, will bring you into opposition to the world just as Jesus was brought into opposition to it. The world crucified Jesus because they couldn't stand Him! There was something in Him that rebuked them and they hated Him for it and finally crucified Him. The world hates the Holy Ghost as bad as they ever hated Jesus, the One from whom He proceeds. Are you sure, brother? You want His help, yes; you want a lot of His benefits, yes; but are you willing to go with Him in His opposition to the easygoing ways of the world? If you are not, you needn't apply for anything more than you have, because you don't want Him; you only think you do!

Again, are you sure that you need to be filled? Can't you get along the way you are? You have been doing fairly well: You pray, you read your Bible, you give to missions, you enjoy singing hymns, you thank God you don't drink or gamble or attend theaters, that you are honest, that you have prayer at home. You are glad about all this. Can't you get along like that? Are you sure you need any more than that? I want to be fair with you. I want to do what Jesus did: He turned around to them when they were following Him and told them the truth. I don't want to take you in under false pretense. "Are you sure you want to follow Me?" He asked, and a great many turned away. But Peter said, "Lord, to whom shall we go? thou hast the words of eternal life." And the crowd that wouldn't turn away was the crowd that made history. The crowd that wouldn't turn back was the crowd that was there when the Holy Ghost came and filled all the place where they were sitting. The crowd that turned back never knew what it was all about.

But maybe you feel in your heart that you just can't go on as you are, that the level of spirituality to which you know yourself called is way beyond you. If you feel that there is something that you must have or your heart will never be satisfied, that there are levels of spirituality, mystic deeps and heights of spiritual communion, purity and power that you have never known, that there is fruit which you know you should bear and do not, victory which you know you should have and have not—I would say, "(Come on," because God has something for you tonight.

There is a spiritual loneliness, an inner aloneness, an inner place where God brings the seeker, where he is as lonely as if there were not another member of the Church anywhere in the world. Ah, when you come there, there is a darkness of mind, an emptiness of heart, a loneliness of soul, but it is preliminary to the daybreak. O God, bring us, somehow, to the daybreak!

Here is how to receive. First, present your body to Him (Rom. 12: 1, 2). God can't fill what He can't have. Now I ask you: Are you ready to present your body with all of its functions and all that it contains—your mind, your personality, your spirit, your love, your ambitions, your all? That is the first thing. That is a simple, easy act—presenting the body. Are you willing to do it?

Now the second thing is to ask (Luke 11: 9-11), and I set aside all theological objections to this text. They say that is not for today. Well, why did the Lord leave it in the Bible then? Why didn't He put it somewhere else; why did He put it where I could see it if He didn't want me to believe it? It is all for us, and if the Lord wanted to do it, He could give it without our asking, but He chooses to have us ask. "Ask of me, and I will give thee" is always God's order; so why not ask?

Acts 5: 32 tells us the third thing to do. God gives His Holy Spirit to them that obey Him. Are you ready to obey and do what you are asked to do? What would that be? Simply to live by the Scriptures as you understand them. Simple, but revolutionary.

The next thing is, have faith (Gal. 3: 2). We receive Him by faith as we receive the Lord in salvation by faith. He comes as a gift of God to us in power. First He comes in some degree and measure when we are converted, otherwise we couldn't be converted. Without Him we couldn't be born again, because we are born of the Spirit. But I am talking about something different now, an advance over that. I am talking about His coming and possessing the full body and mind and life and heart, taking the whole personality over, gently, but directly and bluntly, and making it His, so that we may become a habitation of God through the Spirit.

So now suppose we sing. Let us sing The Comforter Has Come, because He has come. If He hasn't come to your heart in fullness, He will; but He has come to the earth. He is here and ready, when we present our vessel, to fill our vessel if we will ask and believe. Will you do it?

How to Cultivate the Spirit's Companionship

"Can two walk together, except they be agreed?" Amos 3: 3.

Now This is what is known as a rhetorical question; it is equivalent to a positive declaration that two cannot walk together except they be agreed, and for two to walk together they must be in some sense one.

They also have to agree that they want to walk together, and they have to agree that it is to their advantage to travel together. I think you will see that it all adds up to this: For two to walk together voluntarily they must be, in some sense, one.

I am talking now about how we can cultivate the Spirit's fellowship, how we can walk with Him day by day and hour by hour—and you won't object if I say "you." Sometimes we preachers preach in the third person, and you can develop a habit of thinking in the third person. We don't talk about "us"; we talk about "they." I don't like that. I think we ought to get personal about this.

There are some of you who are not ready for this sermon at all. You are trying to face both ways at once. You are trying to take some of this world and to get some of that world over yonder. You are a Christian, but I am talking about an advance upon the first early stages of salvation and the cultivation of the presence of the Holy Ghost, so that He may illuminate and bless and lift and purify and direct your life. You are not ready for this, because you haven't given up all that you might have the All. You want some, but you don't want all; that is the reason you are not ready.

You who have not given up the world will not be able to understand what I am talking about. You want Christianity for its insurance value. You want just what a man wants when he takes out a policy on his life, or his car, or his house. You don't want modernism, because it hasn't any insurance value. You are willing to support this proposition financially. He would be a poor man who would want insurance and not be willing to pay for it. If Jesus Christ died for you on the cross you are very happy about that because it means you won't be brought into judgment, but have passed from death into life. You are willing to live reasonably well, because that is the premium you are paying for the guarantee that God will bless you while you live and take you home to heaven when you die!

You may not be ready because your conception of religion is social and not spiritual. There are people like that. They have watered down the religion of the New Testament until it has no strength in it. They have introduced the water of their own opinion into it, until it has no taste left. They are socially minded. This is as far as it goes with them. People like that may be saved. I am not prepared to say that they are not saved, but I am prepared to say that they are not ready for what I am talking about. The gospel of Christ is essentially spiritual, and Christian truth working upon human souls by the Holy Ghost makes Christian men and women spiritual.

I don't like to say this, but I think that some of you may not be ready for this message because you are more influenced by the world than you are by the New Testament. I am perfectly certain that I could rake up fifteen boxcar loads of fundamentalist Christians this hour in the city of Chicago who are more influenced in their whole outlook by Hollywood than they are by the Lord Jesus Christ. I am positive that much that passes for the gospel in our day is very little more than a very mild case of orthodox religion grafted on to a heart that is sold out to the world in its pleasures and tastes and ambitions.

The kind of teaching that I have been giving has disturbed some people. I am not going to apologize at all, because, necessarily, if I have been traveling along thinking I am all right and there comes a man of God and tells me that there is yet much land to be possessed, it will disturb me. That is the preliminary twinge that comes to the soul that wants to know God. Whenever the Word of God hits us, it disturbs us. So don't be disturbed by the disturbance. Remember that it is quite normal. God has to jar us loose.

But there are some who are prepared. They are those who have made the grand, sweet committal. They have seen heaven draw nearer and earth recede; the things of this world have become less and less attractive, and the things of heaven have begun to pull and pull as the moon pulls at the sea, and they are prepared now. So I am going to give you these few little pointers to help you into a better life.

Point one is that the Holy Spirit is a living person. He is the third Person of the Trinity. He is Himself God, and as a Person, He can be cultivated; He can be wooed and cultivated the same as any person can be. People grow on us, and the Holy Spirit, being a Person, can grow on us.

The second point is: Be engrossed with Jesus Christ. Honor Him. John said: "But this spake he of the Spirit, which they that believe on him should receive: for the Holy Ghost was not yet given; because that Jesus was not yet glorified."

I ask you to note that the Spirit was given when Jesus was glorified. Now that is a principle. Remember that He came and spread Himself out as a flood upon the people because Jesus was glorified. He established a principle, and He will never, never flood the life of any man except the man in whom Jesus is glorified. Therefore, if you dedicate yourself to the glory of Jesus, the Holy Ghost will become the aggressor and will seek to know you and raise you and illumine you and fill you and bless you. Honoring Jesus Christ is doing the things which Jesus told you to do, trusting Him as your All, following Him as your Shepherd, and obeying Him fully.

Let's cultivate the Holy Ghost by honoring the Lord Jesus. As we honor Jesus, the Spirit of God becomes glad within us. He ceases to hold back, He relaxes and becomes intimate and communes and imparts Himself; and the sun comes up and heaven comes near as Jesus Christ becomes our all in all.

To glorify Jesus is the business of the Church, and to glorify Jesus is the work of the Holy Ghost. I can walk with Him when I am doing the same things He is doing, and go the same way He is going and travel at the same speed He is traveling. I must be engrossed with Jesus Christ. I must honor Him. "If any man serve me, him will my Father honour" (John 12: 26). So let's honor the Lord Jesus. Not only theologically, but let's honor Him personally.

The third point is: Let's walk in righteousness. The grace of God that bringeth salvation also teaches the heart that we should deny ungodliness and worldly lusts and live soberly and righteously and godly in this present world. There you have the three dimensions of life. Soberly—that is me. Righteously— that is my fellowman. Godly—that is God. Let us not make the mistake of thinking we can be spiritual and not be good. Let's not make the mistake of thinking we can walk with the Holy Ghost and go a wrong or a dirty or an unrighteous way, for how can two walk together except they be agreed? He is the Holy Spirit, and if I walk an unholy way, how can I fellowship with Him?

The fourth is: Make your thoughts a clean sanctuary. To God, our thoughts are things. Our thoughts are the decorations inside the sanctuary where we live. If our thoughts are purified by the blood of Christ, we are living in a clean room no matter if we are wearing overalls covered with grease. Your thoughts pretty much decide the mood and weather and climate inside your heart, and God considers your thoughts as part of you. Thoughts of peace, thoughts of pity, thoughts of mercy, thoughts of kindness, thoughts of charity, thoughts of God, thoughts of the Son of God-these are pure things, good things, and high things. Therefore, if you would cultivate the Spirit's acquaintance, you must get hold of your thoughts and not allow your mind to be a wilderness in which every kind of unclean beast roams and bird flies. You must have a clean heart.

Point five: Let us seek to know Him in the Word. It is in the Word we will find the Holy Spirit. Don't read too many other things. Some of you will say, "Look who's talking!" Well, go ahead and say it, I don't mind; but I am reading fewer and fewer things as I get older, not because I am losing interest in this great, big, old suffering world, but because I am gaining interest in that other world above. So I say, don't try to know everything. You can't. Find Him in the Word, for the Holy Ghost wrote this Book. He inspired it, and He will be revealed in its pages.

What is the word when we come to the Bible? It is meditate. We are to come to the Bible and meditate. That is what the old saints did. They meditated. They laid the Bible on the old-fashioned handmade chair, got down on the old, scrubbed board floor and meditated on the Word. As they meditated, faith mounted. The Spirit and faith illuminated. They had nothing but a Bible with fine print and narrow margins and poor paper, but they knew their Bible better than some of us with all of our helps. Let's practice the art of Bible meditation.

Now please don't grab that phrase and go out and form a club. Don't do it! Just meditate. That is what we need. We are organized to death already. Let's just be plain Christians. Let's open our Bible, spread it out on the chair, and meditate on it. It will open itself to us, and the Spirit of God will come and brood over it.

So be a Bible meditator. I challenge you: Try it for a month and see how it works. Put away questions and answers and the filling in of blank lines about Noah. Put all that cheap trash away and take a Bible, open it, get on your knees and say, "Father, here I am. Begin to teach me." He will begin to teach you, and He will teach you about Himself and about Jesus and about God and about the Word and about life and death and heaven and hell, and about His own Presence.

I have just one more point: Cultivate the art of recognizing the presence of the Spirit everywhere. Get acquainted with the Holy Ghost and then begin to cultivate His presence. When you wake in the morning, in place of burying your head behind the Tribune, couldn't you get in just a few thoughts of God while you eat your grapefruit?

Remember, cultivating the Holy Ghost's acquaintance is a job. It is something you do, and yet it is so easy and delightful. It is like cultivating your baby's acquaintance. You know when you first look at the little wrinkled fellow, yelling, all mouth, you don't know him. He is a little stranger to you. Then you begin to cultivate him, and he smiles. (It isn't a smile at all. He has colic! You think it is a smile, and it is such a delight.) Pretty soon he wiggles an arm, and you think he is waving at you. Then he gurgles and you think he said "Mama." You get acquainted!

Is this for ministers? This is for ministers, certainly. Is it for housewives? Yes, housewives, and clerks and milkmen and students. If you will thus see it and thus believe it and thus surrender to it, there won't be a secular stone in the pavement. There won't be a common, profane deed that you will ever do. The most menial task can become a priestly ministration when the Holy Ghost takes over and Christ becomes your all in all.

The Christian Book of Mystical Verse

[1963]

INTRODUCTION

The purpose of this book is to bring together in one convenient volume some of the best devotional verse the English language affords, and thus to make available to present day Christians a rich spiritual heritage which the greater number of them for various reasons do not now enjoy.

I have not hesitated to apply the term "mystical" to the material I have collected here, though I readily admit that fewer than half a dozen of the men and women who would be called true mystics in the strict classical sense will be found here. Such names as Eckhart, Ruysbroeck, John of the Cross, Teresa, Rolle, Tauler, Hilton, Francis of Assisi, for instance, are not represented in this volume at all. On the other hand the frequent appearance of such a man as Watts might cause the reader to lift a questioning eyebrow and ask, "Is Watts also among the mystics?"

Well, the answer must be, Of course he is, and so are John Newton and James Montgomery and Reginald Heber and Charles Wesley, as well as many others who might have balked at being called mystics but whose writings, nevertheless, reveal unmistakable traces of purest mysticism and are the better for it. And for that matter the same thing may be said of the inspired writings of such men as Moses and David and Isaiah and Daniel and Paul and John, the works of the latter showing more than traces of the mystical spirit, being indeed charged full with it.

As short a time as, say, forty years ago, the words "mystic" and "mystical" were altogether unacceptable in evangelical circles. Among the gospel churches the words suggested someone who was emotionally unstable, visionary, and worst of all, unsound theologically.

Now there are undoubtedly many persons with a temperamental fondness for the fantastic. These have by nature a strong psychic bent that predisposes them toward the occult; they have also an incredible capacity for self-deception and are ready to accept whatever in the realm of religion is bizarre and prodigious. Such as these have been sometimes called mystics—something they most surely are not.

The word "mystic" as it occurs in the title of this book refers to that personal spiritual experience common to the saints of Bible times and well known to multitudes of persons in the post-Biblical era. I refer to the evangelical mystic who has been brought by the gospel into intimate fellowship with the Godhead. His theology is no less and no more than is taught in the Christian Scriptures. He walks the high road of truth where walked of old prophets and apostles, and where down the centuries walked martyrs, reformers, Puritans, evangelists and missionaires of the cross. He differs from the ordinary orthodox Christian only because he experiences his faith down in the depths of his sentient being while the other does not. He exists in a world of spiritual reality. He is quietly, deeply, and sometimes almost ecstatically aware of the Presence of God in his own nature and in the world around him. His religious experience is something elemental, as old as time and the creation. It is immediate acquaintance with God by union with the Eternal Son. It is to know that which passes knowledge.

The hymns and poems found here are mystical in that they are God-oriented; they begin with God, embrace the worshipping soul and return to God again. And they cover almost the full spectrum of religious feeling: fear, hope, penitence, aspiration, the longing to be holy, yearning after God, gratitude, thanksgiving, pure admiration of the Godhead, love for Christ, worship, praise and adoration. The mood runs from near despair to near ecstasy, and the twin notes of utter sincerity and deepest reverence may be heard throughout.

This is a book for the worshiper rather than, for the student. It has been carefully and lovingly prepared for those God-enamored persons who, while they feel as deeply as the enraptured poet, yet lack the gift that would enable them to express their feelings adequately. Such will sense a kinship with the gifted souls they find on the pages of this book and will join them as they mount on high to pour out their hymns at heaven's gate.

In making these selections I have largely followed my own bent, though I have been guided somewhat by a few simple rules. First, all sentimental verse was excluded, along with everything homey and maudlin. The only healthy emotions are those aroused by great ideas, and even these must be restrained and purified by the Spirit of God or they will spend themselves in weak and sterile rhymes. Of such there is enough in the religious world; I think none will be found in this book.

Second, while the compiler is not unfamiliar with the judgment of hymnologists and literary critics on the larger body of English religious verse, that judgment has been set aside and another adopted for this book. For this reason some of the standard classics have been omitted because I felt they would not contribute to my purpose. Conversely, certain poems of admittedly inferior literary rank have been included because I felt that they would.

Third, everything selected for inclusion in this work had to be judged theologically sound. While considerable latitude was allowed, even welcomed, in doctrinal outlook and emphasis, to be accepted every hymn and poem had to meet the test of faithfulness to the Christian Scriptures.

Though almost everything here is pure lyric poetry and may easily be sung, yet this book is not intended for use in the public assembly. Had I meant it to be so used a wholly different kind of verse would have been chosen for it and the book would have been another sort of book altogether. Everything here is for use in private devotion. I have had in mind not a congregation but the lone individual. For this reason I would respectfully urge the one who may come into possession of this book not to "read" it as he would read another book. Let him try rather to enter into its mood, to capture and be captured by its spirit. How many pages he gets through in a day is of no importance; what one poem or even one single stanza does to him and for him and in him: that is everything.

Admittedly much pure gold has been left out of this treasury. The chief reason is lack of space. I have tried to keep the book small enough to be portable, that its possessor may carry it with him and so turn any bus or train or airplane into a sanctuary. Certainly not all the gold in the world is in this one volume, but what is here is, I believe, true gold of Ophir. I hope many of my fellow Christians will find it to be so.

A. W. Tozer

ADORATION OF THE GODHEAD

ETERNAL POWER!

Eternal Power, whose high abode
Becomes the grandeur of a God:
Infinite lengths beyond the bounds
Where stars revolve their little rounds:

Thee while the first archangel sings,
He hides his face behind his wings:
And ranks of shining thrones around
Fall worshipping, and spread the ground.

Lord, what shall earth and ashes do?
We would adore our Maker too;
From sin and dust to Thee we cry,
The Great, the Holy, and the High.

Earth, from afar, hath heard Thy fame,
And worms have learn'd to lisp Thy Name;
But O! the glories of Thy mind
Leave all our soaring thoughts behind.

God is in heaven, and men below:
Be short our times; our words be few:
A solemn reverence checks our songs,
And praise sits silent on our tongues.

—*Isaac Watts, 1674-1748*

LORD OF ALL BEING

Lord of all being, throned afar,
Thy glory flames from sun and star;
Center and soul of every sphere,
Yet to each loving heart how near.

Sun of our life, Thy quickening ray
Sheds on our path the glow of day;
Star of our hope, Thy softened light
Cheers the long watches of the night.

Our midnight is Thy smile withdrawn;
Our noontide is Thy gracious dawn;
Our rainbow arch, Thy mercy's sign;
All, save the clouds of sin, are Thine.

Lord of all life, below, above,
Whose light is truth, whose warmth is love,
Before Thy ever blazing throne
We ask no luster of our own.

Grant us Thy truth to make us free,
And kindling hearts that burn for Thee,
Till all Thy living altars claim
One holy light, one heavenly flame.

—Oliver Wendell Holmes, 1809-1894

ADORATION

Almighty One! I bend in dust before Thee;
Even so veiled cherubs bend;
In calm and still devotion I adore Thee,
All-wise, all-present Friend!

Thou to the earth its emerald robes hast given,
Or curtained it in snow;
And the bright sun, and the soft moon in heaven,
Before Thy presence bow.

Thou Power sublime! whose throne is firmly seated
On stars and glowing suns;
O, could I praise Thee,—could my soul, elated,
Waft Thee seraphic tones, —
Had I the lyres of angels, —could I bring Thee
An offering worthy Thee, —
In what bright notes of glory would I sing Thee,
Blest notes of ecstasy!

Eternity! Eternity! how solemn,
How terrible the sound!
Here, leaning on thy promises, —a column
Of strength, —may I be found,
O, let my heart be ever Thine, while beating,
As when 'twill cease to beat!
Be Thou my portion, till that awful meeting
When I my God shall greet!

—Sir John Bowring, 1792-1872

THE UNITY OF GOD

One God! one Majesty!
There is no God but Thee!
Unbounded, unextended Unity!

Awful in unity,
O God! we worship Thee,
More simply one, because supremely Three!

Dread, unbeginning One!
Single, yet not alone,
Creation hath not set Thee on a higher throne.

Unfathomable Sea!
All life is out of Thee,
And Thy life is Thy blissful Unity.

All things that from Thee run,
All works that Thou hast done,
Thou didst in honour of Thy being One.

And by Thy being One,
Ever by that alone,
Couldst Thou do, and doest, what Thou hast done.

We from Thy oneness come,
Beyond it cannot roam,
And in Thy oneness find our one eternal home.

Blest be Thy Unity!
All joys are one to me,—
The joy that there can be no other God than Thee!

—Frederick William Faber, 1814-1863

THE HOLY TRINITY

O Blessed Trinity!
Thy children dare to lift their hearts to Thee,
And bless Thy triple Majesty!
Holy Trinity!
Blessed Equal Three,
One God, we praise Thee.

O Blessed Trinity!
Holy, unfathomable, infinite,
Thou art all Life and Love and Light.
Holy Trinity!
Blessed Equal Three,
One God, we praise Thee.

O Blessed Trinity!
God of a thousand attributes! we see
That there is no one good but Thee.
Holy Trinity!
Blessed Equal Three,
One God, we praise Thee.

O Blessed Trinity!
In our astonished reverence we confess
Thine uncreated loveliness.
Holy Trinity!
Blessed Equal Three,
One God, we praise Thee.

O Blessed Trinity!
O simplest Majesty! O Three in One!
Thou art for ever God alone.
Holy Trinity!
Blessed Equal Three,
One God, we praise Thee.

O Blessed Trinity!
The Fountain of the Godhead, in repose,
For ever rests, for ever flows.
Holy Trinity!
Blessed Equal Three,
One God, we praise Thee.

O Blessed Trinity!
O Unbegotten Father! give us tears
To quench our love, to calm our fears.
Holy Trinity!
Blessed Equal Three,
One God, we praise Thee.

O Blessed Trinity!
Bright Son! who art the Father's mind displayed,
Thou art begotten and not made.
Holy Trinity!
Blessed Equal Three,
One God, we praise Thee.

O Blessed Trinity!
Coequal Spirit! wondrous Paraclete!
By Thee the Godhead is complete.
Holy Trinity!
Blessed Equal Three,
One God, we praise Thee.

O Blessed Trinity!
We praise Thee, bless Thee, worship Thee as one.
Yet Three are on the single Throne.
Holy Trinity!
Blessed Equal Three,
One God, we praise Thee.

O Blessed Trinity!
In the deep darkness of prayer's stillest night
We worship Thee blinded with light.
Holy Trinity!
Blessed Equal Three,
One God, we praise Thee.

O Blessed Trinity!
Oh would that we could die of love for Thee,
Incomparable Trinity!
Holy Trinity!
Blessed Equal Three,
One God, we praise Thee.

—Frederick William Faber, 1814-1863

MAJESTY DIVINE!

Full of glory, full of wonders,
Majesty Divine!
Mid Thine everlasting thunders
How Thy lightnings shine!
Shoreless Ocean! who shall sound Thee?
Thine own eternity is round Thee,
Majesty Divine!

Timeless, spaceless, single, lonely,
Yet sublimely Three,
Thou art grandly, always, only
God in Unity!
Lone in grandeur, lone in glory,
Who shall tell Thy wondrous story,
Awful Trinity?

Speechlessly, without beginning,
Sun that never rose!
Vast, adorable, and winning,
Day that hath no close!
Bliss from Thine own glory tasting,
Everliving, everlasting,
Life that never grows!

Thine own Self for ever filling
With self-kindled flame,
In Thyself Thou art distilling
Unctions without name!
Without worshipping of creatures
Without veiling of Thy features,
God always the same!

In Thy praise of Self untiring
Thy perfections shine;
Self-sufficient, self-admiring,—
Such life must be Thine;—
Glorifying Self, yet blameless
With a sanctity all shameless
It is so divine!

Mid Thine uncreated morning,
Like a trembling star
I behold creation's dawning
Glimmering from afar;
Nothing giving, nothing taking,
Nothing changing, nothing breaking,
Waiting at time's bar!

I with life and love diurnal
See myself in Thee,
All embalmed in love eternal,
Floating in Thy sea:
'Mid Thine uncreated whiteness
I behold Thy glory's brightness
Feed itself on me.

Splendours upon splendours beaming
Change and intertwine;
Glories over glories streaming
All translucent shine!
Blessings, praises adorations
Greet Thee from the trembling nations
Majesty Divine!

—Frederick William Faber, 1814-1863

THE VISION OF THE GODHEAD

Unchanging and Unchangeable, before angelic eyes,
The Vision of the Godhead in its tranquil beauty lies;
And, like a city lighted up all gloriously within,
Its countless lustres glance and gleam, and sweetest worship win.
On the Unbegotten Father, awful well-spring of the Three,
On the Sole Begotten Son's coequal Majesty.
On Him eternally breathed forth from Father and from Son.
The spirits gaze with fixed amaze, and unreckoned ages run.

Chorus:
Myriad, myriad angels raise
Happy hymns of wondering praise,
Ever through eternal days,
Before the Holy Trinity,
One Undivided Three!

Still the Fountain of the Godhead give the forth eternal being:
Still begetting, unbegotten, still His own perfection seeing,
Still limiting His own loved Self with His dear coequal Spirit,
No change comes o'er that blissful Life, no shadow passeth near it.
And beautiful dread Attributes, all manifold and bright,
Now thousands seem, now lose themselves in one self-living light;
And far in that deep Life of God, in harmony complete,
Like crowned kings, all opposite perfections take their seat
And in that ungrowing vision nothing deepens, nothing brightens,
But the living Life of God perpetually lightens;
And created life is nothing but a radiant shadow fleeing
From the unapproached lustres of that Unbeginning Being;

Spirits wise and deep have watched that everlasting Ocean,
And never o'er its lucid field hath rippled faintest motion;
In glory undistinguished never have the Three seemed One,
Nor ever in divided streams the Single Essence run.

There reigns the Eternal Father, in His lone prerogatives,
And, in the Father's Mind, the Son, all self-existing, lives,
With Him, their mutual Jubilee, that deepest depth of love,
Lifegiving Life of two-fold source, the many gifted Dove!
O Bountiful! O Beautiful! can Power or Wisdom add
Fresh features to a life, so munificent and glad?
Can even uncreated Love, ye angels! give a hue
Which can ever make the Unchanging and Unchangeable look new?

The Mercy of the Merciful is equal to Their Might,
As wondrous as Their Love, and as Their Wisdom bright!
As They, who out of nothing called creation at the first,
In everlasting purposes Their own design had nursed,—
As They, who in their solitude, Three Persons, once abode,
Vouchsafed of Their abundance to become creation's God,—
What They owed not to Themselves They stooped to owe to man,
And pledged Their glory to him, in an unimaginable plan.

See! deep within the glowing depth of that Eternal Light.
What change hath come, what vision new transports angelic sight?
A creature can it be, in uncreated bliss?
A novelty in God? Oh what nameless thing is this?
The beauty of the Father's Power is o'er it brightly shed,
The sweetness of the Spirit's Love is unction on its head;
In the wisdom of the Son it plays its wondrous part,
While it lives the loving life of a real Human heart!

A Heart that hath a Mother, and a treasure of red blood,
A Heart that man can pray to, and feed upon for food!
In the brightness of the Godhead is its marvellous abode,
A change in the Unchanging, creation touching God!
Ye spirits blest, in endless rest, who on that Vision gaze,
Salute the Sacred Heart with all your worshipful amaze,
And adore, while with ecstatic skill the Three in One ye scan,
The Mercy that hath planted there that blessed Heart of Man!

All tranquilly, all tranquilly, doth that Blissful Vision last,
And Its brightness o'er immortalized creation will it cast;
Ungrowing and unfading, Its pure Essence doth it keep,
In the deepest of those depths where all are infinitely deep;
Unchanging and Unchangeable as It hath ever been,
As It was before that Human heart was there by angels seen,
So is it at this very hour, so will it ever be,
With that Human Heart within It, beating hot with love of me!

Chorus:

Myriad, myriad angels raise
Happy hymns of wondering praise,
Ever through eternal days,
Before the Holy Trinity,
One Undivided Three!

—Frederick William Faber, 1814-1863

THE THOUGHT OF GOD

The thought of God, the thought of Thee,
Who liest in my heart,
And yet beyond imagined space
Outstretched and present art,—

The thought of Thee, above, below,
Around me and within,
Is more to me than health and wealth,
Or love of kith and kin.

The thought of God is like the tree
Beneath whose shade I lie,
And watch the fleets of snowy clouds
Sail o'er the silent sky.

'Tis like that soft invading light,
Which in all darkness shines,
The thread that through life's sombre web
In golden pattern twines.

It is a thought which ever makes
Life's sweetest smiles from tears,
And is a daybreak to our hopes,
A sunset to our fears;

One while it bids the tears to flow,
Then wipes them from the eyes,
Most often fills our souls with joy,
And always sanctifies.

Within a thought so great, our souls
Little and modest grow,
And, by its vastness awed, we learn
The art of walking slow.

The wild flower on the mossy ground
Scarce bends its pliant form,
When overhead the autumnal wood
Is thundering like a storm.

So is it with our humbled souls
Down in the thought of God,
Scarce conscious in their sober peace
Of the wild storms abroad.

To think of Thee is almost prayer,
And is outspoken praise;
And pain can even passive thoughts
To actual worship raise.

O Lord! I live always in pain,
My life's sad undersong,
Pain in itself not hard to bear,
But hard to bear so long.

Little sometimes weighs more than much,
When it has no relief;
A joyless life is worse to bear
Than one of active grief.

And yet, O Lord! a suffering life
One grand ascent may dare;
Penance, not self-imposed, can make
The whole of life a prayer.

All murmurs he inside Thy Will
Which are to Thee addressed;
To suffer for Thee is our work,
To think of Thee our rest.

—Frederick William Faber, 1814-1863

THE GREATNESS OF GOD

O Majesty unspeakable and dread!
Wert Thou less mighty than Thou art,
Thou wert, O Lord! too great for our belief,
Too little for our heart.

Thy greatness would seem monstrous by the side
Of creatures frail and undivine;
Yet they would have a greatness of their own
Free and apart from Thine.

Such grandeur were but a created thing,
A spectre, terror, and a grief,
Out of all keeping with a world so calm,
Oppressing our belief.

But greatness, which is infinite makes room
For all things in its lap to lie;
We should be crushed by a magnificence
Short of infinity.

It would outgrow us from the face of things,
Still prospering as we decayed,
And, like a tyrannous rival, it would feed
Upon the wrecks it made.

But what is infinite must be a home,
A shelter for the meanest fife,
Where it is free to reach its greatest growth
Far from the touch of strife.

We share in what is infinite: 'tis ours,
For we and it alike are Thine;
What I enjoy, great God! by right of Thee
Is more than doubly mine.

Thus doth Thy hospitable greatness lie
Outside us like a boundless sea;
We cannot lose ourselves where all is home,
Nor drift away from Thee.

Out on that sea we are in harbour still,
And scarce advert to winds and tides,
Like ships that ride at anchor, with the waves
Flapping against their sides.

Thus doth Thy grandeur make us grand ourselves;
'Tis goodness bids us fear;
Thy greatness makes us brave as children are,
When those they love are near.

Great God, our lowliness takes heart to play
Beneath the shadow of Thy state;
The only comfort of our littleness
Is that Thou art so great.

Then on Thy grandeur I will lay me down;
Already life is heaven for me;
No cradled child more softly lies than I,—
Come soon, Eternity!

—Frederick William Faber, 1814-1863

THE ETERNITY OF GOD

O Lord! my heart is sick,
Sick of this everlasting change;
And life runs tediously quick
Through its unresting race and varied range:
Change finds no likeness to itself in Thee,
And wakes no echo in Thy mute Eternity.

Dear Lord! my heart is sick
Of this perpetual lapsing time,
So slow in grief, in joy so quick,
Yet ever casting shadows so sublime;
Time of all creatures is least like to Thee,
And yet it is our share of Thine eternity.

O change and time are storms
For lives so thin and frail as ours;
For change the work of grace deforms
With love that soils, and help that overpowers;
And time is strong, and, like some chafing sea,
It seems to fret the shores of Thine eternity.

Weak, weak, forever weak!
We cannot hold what we possess;
Youth cannot find, age will not seek,
O weakness is the heart's worst weariness:
But weakest hearts can lift their thoughts to Thee;
It makes us strong to think of Thine eternity.

Thou hadst no youth, great God,
An Unbeginning End Thou art;
Thy glory in itself abode,
And still abides in its own tranquil heart:
No age can heap its outward years on Thee:
Dear God! Thou art Thyself Thine own eternity!

Without an end or bound
Thy life lies all outspread in light;
Our lives feel Thy life all around,
Making our weakness strong, our darkness bright;
Yet is it neither wilderness nor sea,
But the calm gladness of a full eternity.

Oh Thou art very great
To set Thyself so far above!
But we partake of Thine estate,
Established in Thy strength and in Thy love:
That love hath made eternal room for me
In the sweet vastness of its own eternity.

Oh Thou art very meek
To overshade Thy creatures thus!
Thy grandeur is the shade we seek:
To be eternal is Thy use to us:
Ah Blessed God! what joy it is to me
To lose all thought of self in Thine eternity.

Self-wearied, Lord! I come;
For I have lived my life too fast:
Now that years bring me nearer home
Grace must be slowly used to make it last;
When my heart beats too quick I think of Thee,
And of the leisure of Thy long eternity.

Farewell, vain joys of earth!
Farewell, all love that is not His!
Dear God! be Thou my only mirth,
Thy majesty my single timid bliss!
Oh in the bosom of eternity
Thou does not weary of Thyself, nor we of Thee!

—Frederick William Faber, 1814-1863

THE FEAR OF GOD

My fear of Thee, O Lord, exults
Like life within my veins,
A fear which rightly claims to be
One of love's sacred pains.

Thy goodness to Thy saints of old
An awful thing appeared;
For were Thy majesty less good
Much less would it be feared.

There is no joy the soul can meet
Upon life's various road
Like the sweet fear that sits and shrinks
Under the eye of God.

A special joy is in all love
For objects we revere;
Thus joy in God will always be
Proportioned to our fear.

Oh Thou art greatly to be feared,
Thou art so prompt to bless!
The dread to miss such love as Thine
Makes fear but love's excess.

The fulness of Thy mercy seems
To fill both land and sea;
If we can break through bounds so vast,
How exiled shall we be!

For grace is fearful, which each hour
Our path in life has crossed;
If it were rarer, it might be
Less easy to be lost.

But fear is love, and love is fear,
And in and out they move;
But fear is an intenser joy
Than mere unfrightened love.

When most I fear Thee, Lord! then most
Familiar I appear;
And I am in my soul most free,
When I am most in fear.

I should not love Thee as I do,
If love might make more free;
Its very sweetness would be lost
In greater liberty.

I feel Thee most a father, when
I fancy Thee most near:
And Thou comest not so nigh in love
As Thou comest, Lord! in fear.

They love Thee little, if at all,
Who do not fear Thee much;
If love is Thine attraction, Lord!
Fear is Thy very touch.

Love could not love Thee half so much
If it found Thee not so near;
It is thy nearness, which makes love
The perfectness of fear.

We fear because Thou art so good,
And because we can sin;
And when we make most show of love,
We are trembling most within.

And Father! when to us in heaven
Thou shalt Thy Face unveil,
Then more than ever will our souls
Before Thy goodness quail.

Our blessedness will be to bear
The sight of Thee so near,
And thus eternal love will be
But the ecstasy of fear.

—Frederick William Faber, 1814-1863

THE ETERNAL FATHER

Father! the sweetest, dearest Name.
That men or angels know!
Fountain of life, that had no fount
From which itself could flow!

Thy life is one unwearing day;
Before its Now Thou hast
No varied future yet unlived,
No lapse of changeless past.

Thou comest not, Thou goest not;
Thou wert not, wilt not be;
Eternity is but a thought
By which we think of Thee.

No epochs lie behind Thy life;
Thou holdst Thy life of none:
No other life is by Thy side;
Thine is supremely lone.

Far upward in the timeless past,
Ere form or space had come,
We see Thee by Thine own dread light,
Thyself Thine only home.

Thy vastness is not young or old;
Thy life hath never grown;
No time can measure out Thy days.
No space can make Thy throne.

Thy life is deep within Thyself,
Sole Unbegotten Sire!
But Son and Spirit flow from Thee
In coeternal fire.

They flow from Thee, They rest in Thee,
As in a Father's Breast-
Processions of eternal love,
Pulses of eternal rest!

That They in majesty should reign
Coequal, Sire! with Thee,
But magnifies the singleness
Of Thy paternity.

Their uncreated glories, Lord!
With Thine own glory shine;
Thy glory as the Father needs
That Theirs should equal Thine.

All things are equal in Thy life:
Thou joyst to be alone,
To have no sire, and yet to have
A coeternal Son.

Thy Spirit is Thy jubilee;
Thy Word is Thy delight;
Thou givest Them to equal Thee
In glory and in might.

Thou art too great to keep unshared
Thy grand eternity;
They have it as Thy gift to Them,
Which is no gift to Thee.

We too, like Thy coequal Word,
Within Thy lap may rest:
We too, like Thine Eternal Dove,
May nestle in Thy Breast.

Lone Fountain of the Godhead! hail!
Person most dread and dear!
I thrill with frightened joy to feel
Thy fatherhood so near.

Lost in Thy greatness, Lord! I live,
As in some gorgeous maze;
Thy sea of unbegotten light
Blinds me, and yet I gaze.

For Thy grandeur is all tenderness,
All motherlike and meek;
The hearts that will not come to it
Humbling itself to seek.

Thou feign'st to be remote, and speakst
As if from far above,
That fear may make more bold with Thee
And be beguiled to love.

On earth Thou hidest, not to scare
The children with Thy light,
Then showest us Thy Face in heaven,
When we can bear the sight.

All fathers learn their craft from Thee;
All loves are shadows cast
From the beautiful eternal hills
Of Thine unbeginning past.

—*Frederick William Faber, 1814-1863*

THE ETERNAL GENERATION OF THE SON

Amid the eternal silences
God's endless Word was spoken;
None heard but He who always spake,
And the silence was unbroken.

Chorus.

Oh marvellous! Oh worshipful!
No song or sound is heard,
But everywhere and every hour,
In love, in wisdom, and in power,
The Father speaks His dear Eternal Word.

For ever in the eternal land
The glorious day is dawning;
For ever is the Father's Light
Like an endless outspread morning.

From the Father's vast tranquillity,
In light coequal glowing
The kingly consubstantial Word
Is unutterably flowing.

For ever climbs that Morning Star
Without ascent or motion;
For ever is its daybreak shed
On the Spirit's boundless ocean.

O Word! who fitly can adore
Thy Birth and Thy Relation,
Lost in the impenetrable light
Of Thine awful Generation?

Thy Father clasps Thee evermore
In unspeakable embraces,
While angels tremble as they praise,
And shroud their dazzled faces.

And oh! in what abyss of love,
So fiery yet so tender,
The Holy Ghost encircles Thee
With His uncreated splendour!

O Word! O dear and gentle Word!
Thy creatures kneel before Thee,
And in ecstacies of timid love
Delightedly adore Thee.

Hail choicest mystery of God!
Hail wondrous Generation!
The Father's self-sufficient rest!
The Spirit's jubilation!

Dear Person! dear beyond all words,
Glorious beyond all telling!
Oh with what songs of silent love
Our ravished hearts are swelling!

Chorus.

O! marvellous! O worshipful!
No song or sound is heard,
But everywhere and every hour,
In love, in wisdom, and in power,
The Father speaks His dear Eternal Word.
      —*FREDERICK WILLIAM FABER, 1814-1863*

THE HOLY SPIRIT

Fountain of Love! Thyself true God!
Who through eternal days
From Father and from Son hast flowed
In uncreated ways!

O Majesty unspeakable!
O Person all divine!
How in the Threefold Majesty
Doth Thy Procession shine!

Fixed in the Godhead's awful light
Thy fiery Breath doth move;
Thou art a wonder by Thyself
To worship and to love!

Proceeding, yet of equal age
With those whose love Thou art:
Proceeding, yet distinct, from those
From whom Thou seem'st to part.

And undivided Nature shared
With Father and with Son;
A Person by Thyself; with Them
Thy simple essence One;

Bond art Thou of the other Twain!
Omnipotent and free!
The consummating Love of God!
The Limit of the Three!

Thou limitest infinity,
Thyself all infinite;
The Godhead lives, and loves, and rests,
In Thine eternal light.

I dread Thee, Unbegotten Love!
True God! sole Fount of Grace!
And now before Thy Blessed throne
My sinful self abase.

Ocean, wide-flowing Ocean, Thou,
Of uncreated Love;
I tremble as within my soul
I feel Thy waters move.

Thou art a sea without a shore;
Awful, immense Thou art;
A sea which can contract itself
Within my narrow heart.

And yet Thou art a haven too
Out on the shoreless sea,
A harbor that can hold full well
Shipwrecked Humanity.

Thou art an unborn Breath outbreathed
On angels and on men,
Subduing all things to Thyself,
We know not how or when.

Thou art a God of fire, that doth
Create while He consumes!
A God of light, whose rays on earth
Darken where He illumes!

All things! dread Spirit! to Thy praise
Thy Presence doth transmute;
Evil itself Thy glory bears,
Its one abiding fruit!

O Light! O Love! O very God
I dare no longer gaze
Upon Thy wondrous attributes,
And their mysterious ways.

O Spirit, beautiful and dread!
My heart is fit to break
With love of all Thy tenderness
For us poor sinners' sake.

Thy love of Jesus I adore;
My comfort this shall be,
That, when I serve my dearest Lord,
That service worships Thee!

—FREDERICK WILLIAM FABER, 1814-1863

PENTECOST

He comes! He comes! that mighty Breath
From heaven's eternal shores;
His uncreated freshness fills
His bride as she adores.

Earth quakes before that rushing blast,
Heaven echoes back the sound,
And mightily the tempest wheels
That Upper Room around.

One moment—and the silentness
Was breathless as the grave;
The fluttered earth forgot to quake,
The troubled trees to wave.

One moment—and the Spirit hung
O'er them with dread desire;
Then broke upon the heads of all
In cloven tongues of fire.

What gifts He gave those chosen men
Past ages can display;
Nay more, their vigour still inspires
The weakness of today.

Those tongues still speak within the Church,
That Fire is undecayed;
Its well-spring was that Upper Room,
Where the disciples met and prayed.

The Spirit came into the Church
With His unfailing power;
He is the Living Heart that beats
Within her at this hour.

Speak gently then of Church and Saints,
Lest you His ways reprove;
The Heat, the Pulses of the Church
Are God's Eternal Love.

Oh let us fall and worship Him,
The Love of Sire and Son,
The Consubstantial Breath of God,
The Coeternal One!

Ah! see, how like the Incarnate Word,
His Blessed Self He lowers,
To dwell with us invisibly,
And make His riches ours.

Most tender Spirit! Mighty God!
Sweet must Thy Presence be,
If loss of Jesus can be gain,
So long as we have Thee!

—FREDERICK WILLIAM FABER, 1814-1863

Devotional Meditations on the Cross of Christ

IF SWEET THE MOMENTS, RICH IN BLESSING

Sweet the moments, rich in blessing,
Which before the Cross I spend;
Life and health and peace possessing
From the sinner's dying Friend.

Truly blessed is this station,
Low before His Cross to lie;
While I see divine compassion
Beaming in His languid eye.

Love and grief my heart dividing,
With my tears His feet I'll bathe;
Constant still in faith abiding,
Life deriving from His death.

For Thy sorrows we adore Thee—
For the griefs that wrought our peace—
Gracious Saviour! we implore Thee,
In our hearts Thy love increase.

—*WALTER SHIRLEY et al., 1725-1786*

RIDE ON! RIDE ON IN MAJESTY!

Ride on! ride on in majesty!
Ride on! ride on in majesty!
Hark! all the tribes "Hosanna" cry:
O Saviour meek, pursue Thy road
With palms and scattered garments strowed.

Ride on! ride on in majesty!
In lowly pomp ride on to die:
O Christ, Thy triumphs now begin
O'er captive death and conquered sin.

Ride on! ride on in majesty!
The winged squadrons of the sky
Look down with sad and wondering eyes
To see the approaching sacrifice.

Ride on! Ride on in majesty!
Thy last and fiercest strife is nigh;
The Father on His sapphire throne
Awaits His own anointed Son.

Ride on! ride on in majesty!
In lowly pomp ride on to die;
Bow Thy meek head to mortal pain,
Then take, O God, Thy power and reign.

—*HENRY HART MILMAN, 1791-1868*

WOULD JESUS HAVE THE SINNER DIE?

Would Jesus have the sinner die?
Why hangs He then on yonder tree?
What means that strange expiring cry?
(Sinners, He prays for you and me;)
Forgive them, Father, O forgive!
They know not that by Me they live.

Jesus, descended from above,
Our loss of Eden to retrieve,
Great God of universal love,
If all the world through Thee may live,
In us a quick'ning spirit be,
And witness Thou hast died for me.

Thou loving, all-atoning Lamb, —
Thee, by Thy painful agony,
Thy bloody sweat, Thy grief and shame,
Thy cross and passion on the tree,
Thy precious death and life—I pray,
Take all, take all my sins away.

O let Thy love my heart constrain, —
Thy love, for every sinner free, —
That every fallen son of man
May taste the grace that found out me;
That all mankind with me may prove
Thy sov'reign, everlasting love.

—CHARLES WESLEY, 1707-1767

HE DIES! THE FRIEND OF SINNERS DIES!

He dies! the Friend of sinners dies!
Lo! Salem's daughters weep around;
A solemn darkness veils the skies,
A sudden trembling shakes the ground:
Come, saints, and drop a tear or two
For Him who groan'd beneath your load;
He shed a thousand drops for you, —
A thousand drops of richer blood.

Here's love and grief beyond degree:
The Lord of glory dies for man!
But lo! what sudden joys we see:
Jesus, the dead, revives again.
The rising God forsakes the tomb;
(In vain the tomb forbids His rise;)
Cherubic legions guard Him home,
And shout Him welcome to the skies.

Break off your tears, ye saints, and tell
How high your great Deliv'rer reigns;
Sing how He spoil'd the hosts of hell,
And led the monster death in chains:
Say, Live forever, wondrous King!
Born to redeem, and strong to save;
Then ask the monster, Where's thy sting?
And, Where's thy vict'ry, boasting grave?

—*ISAAC WATRS, 1674-1748*

BEFORE THE CROSS

My Lord, my Master, at Thy feet adoring,
I see Thee bowed beneath Thy load of woe:
For me, a sinner, is Thy life-blood pouring;
For Thee, my Saviour, scarce my tears will flow.

Thine own disciple to the Jews has sold Thee,
With friendship's kiss and loyal word he came;
How oft of faithful love my lips have told Thee,
While Thou hast seen my falsehood and my shame!

With taunts and scoffs they mock what seems Thy weakness,
With blows and outrage adding pain to pain;
Thou art unmoved and steadfast in Thy meekness;
When I am wronged how quickly I complain!

My Lord, my Saviour, when I see Thee wearing
Upon Thy bleeding brow the crown of thorn,
Shall I for pleasure live, or shrink from bearing
Whate'er my lot may be of pain or scorn?

O Victim of Thy love, O pangs most healing,
O saving death, O wounds that I adore,
O shame most glorious! Christ, before Thee kneeling,
I pray Thee keep me Thine for evermore.

—*From the French of JACQUES BRIDAINE, 1701-1767*
Tr. THOMAS BENSON POLLOCK, 1836-1896

O SACRED HEAD, NOW WOUNDED

O Sacred Head, now wounded,
With grief and shame weighed down,
Now scornfully surrounded
With thorns, Thine only crown;
O sacred Head, what glory,
What bliss, till now was Thine!
Yet though despised and gory,
I joy to call Thee mine.

What Thou, my Lord, hast suffered
Was all for sinners' gain;
Mine, mine was the transgression,
But Thine the deadly pain;
Lo, here I fall, my Saviour!
'Tis I deserve Thy place;
Look on me with Thy favor,
Vouchsafe to me Thy grace.

What language shall I borrow
To thank Thee, dearest Friend,
For this Thy dying sorrow,
Thy pity without end?
Oh, make me Thine forever;
And should I fainting be,
Lord, let me never, never
Outlive my love to Thee!

Be near me when I'm dying;
Oh, show Thy Cross to me!
And for my succor flying;
Come, Lord, and set me free!
These eyes, new faith receiving,
From Jesus shall not move;
For he who dies believing,
Dies safely, through Thy love.

—BERNARD OF CLAIRVAUX, 1091-1153
Tr. PAUL GERHARDT, 1607-1676
English tr., JAMES WADDELL ALEXANDER, 1859-1904

NOT ALL THE BLOOD OF BEASTS

Not all the blood of beasts,
On Jewish altars slain,
Could give the guilty conscience peace,
Or wash away the stain.

But Christ, the heavenly Lamb,
Takes all our sins away;

A sacrifice of nobler name,
And richer blood than they.

My faith would lay her hand
On that dear head of Thine,
While like a penitent I stand,
And there confess my sin.

My soul looks back, to see
The burdens Thou didst bear,
When hanging on the cursed tree,
And hopes her guilt was there.

Believing, we rejoice
To see the curse remove;
We bless the Lamb with cheerful voice,
And sing His bleeding love.

—ISAAC WATTS, 1674-1748

Penitential Reflections on Our Sins

MY SINS, MY SAVIOUR!

My sins, my sins, my Saviour!
They take such hold on me,
I am not able to look up,
Save only Christ to Thee;
In Thee is all forgiveness,
In Thee abundant grace,
My shadow and my sunshine
The brightness of Thy face.

My sins, my sins, my Saviour!
How sad on Thee they fall;
Seen through Thy gentle patience,
I ten-fold feel them all;
I know they are forgiven,
But still, their pain to me
Is all the grief and anguish
They laid, my Lord, on Thee.

My sins, my sins, my Saviour!
Their guilt I never knew
Till with Thee in the desert
I near Thy passion drew;
Till with Thee in the garden
I heard Thy pleading pray'r,
And saw the sweat-drops bloody
That told Thy sorrow there.

Therefore my songs, my Saviour,
E'en in this time of woe,
Shall tell of all Thy goodness
To suffering man below;
Thy goodness and Thy favor,
Whose presence from above
Rejoice those hearts my Saviour,
That live in Thee alone.

—*JOHN S. B. MONSELL, 1811-1875*

HAVE MERCY, GOD MOST HIGH

Have mercy on us, God Most High!
Who lift our hearts to Thee;
Have mercy on us worms of earth,
Most holy Trinity!

Most ancient of all mysteries!
Before Thy throne we lie;
Have mercy now most merciful,
Most holy Trinity!

When heaven and earth were yet unmade,
When time was yet unknown,
Thou in Thy bliss and majesty
Didst live and love alone!

Thou wert not born; there was no fount
From which Thy Being flowed;
There is no end which Thou canst reach:
But Thou art simply God.

How wonderful creation is,
The work that Thou didst bless,
And, oh! what then must Thou be like,
Eternal Loveliness?

How beautiful the Angels are,
The Saints how bright in bliss;
But with Thy beauty, Lord! compared,
How dull, how poor is this!

No wonder Saints have died of love,
No wonder hearts can break,
Pure hearts that once have learned to love
God for His own dear sake.

O listen, then, Most Pitiful!
To Thy poor creature's heart;
It blesses Thee that Thou art God,
That Thou art what Thou art!

Most ancient of all mysteries!
Still at Thy throne we lie;
Have mercy now, most merciful,
Most holy Trinity!

—FREDERICK WILLIAM FABER, 1814-1863

O LORD, I AM ASHAMED TO SEEK THY FACE

O Lord, I am ashamed to seek Thy Face
As tho' I loved Thee as Thy saints love Thee:
Yet turn from those Thy lovers, look on me,
Disgrace me not with uttermost disgrace;
But pour on me ungracious, pour Thy grace
To purge my heart and bid my will go free,
Till I too taste Thy hidden Sweetness, see
Thy hidden Beauty in the holy place.
O Thou Who callest sinners to repent,
Call me Thy sinner unto penitence,
For many sins grant me the greater love:
Set me above the waterfloods, above
Devil and shifting world and fleshly sense,
Thy Mercy's all-amazing monument.

—*CHRISTINA ROSSETTI, 1830-1894*

SCOURGE, BUT RECEIVE ME

Good Lord, today
I scarce find breath to say:
Scourge, but receive me.
For stripes are hard to bear, but worse
Thy intolerable curse;
So do not leave me.

Good Lord, lean down
In pity, tho' Thou frown;
Smite, but retrieve me:
For so Thou hold me up to stand
And kiss Thy smiting hand,
It less will grieve me.

—*CHRISTINA ROSSETTI, 1830-1894*

Rejoicing in Forgiveness and Justification

SONG OF ASSURANCE

Now I have found the ground wherein
Sure my soul's anchor may remain,
The wounds of Jesus, for my sin
Before the world's foundation slain;
Whose mercy shall unshaken stay,
When heaven and earth are fled away.

Father, Thine everlasting grace
Our scanty thought surpasses far:
Thy heart still melts with tenderness.
Thy arms of love still open are,
Returning sinners to receive,
That mercy they may taste and live.

O Love, Thou bottomless abyss,
My sins are swallowed up in Thee!
Covered is my unrighteousness,
Nor spot of guilt remains on me,
While Jesus' blood, through earth and skies,
Mercy, free, boundless mercy, cries.

With faith I plunge me in this sea;
Here is my hope, my joy, my rest;
Hither, when hell assails, I flee,
I look into my Saviour's breast;
Away, sad doubt, and anxious fear!
Mercy is all that's written there.

Though waves and storms go o'er my head,
Though strength, and health, and friends be gone,
Though joys be withered all and dead,
Though every comfort be withdrawn,
On this my steadfast soul relies, —
Father, Thy mercy never dies.

Fixed on this ground will I remain,
Though my heart fail, and flesh decay;
This anchor shall my soul sustain,
When earth's foundations melt away;
Mercy's full power I then shall prove,
Loved with an everlasting love.

—*JOHANN ANDREAS ROTHE, 1688-1758*
Tr. JOHN WESLEY, 1703-1791

A GOOD CONFESSION

The chains that have bound me are flung to the wind,
By the mercy of God the poor slave is set free;
And the strong grace of heaven breathes fresh o'er the mind,
Like the bright winds of summer that gladden the sea.

There was nought in God's world half so dark or so vile
As the sin and the bondage that fettered my soul;
There was nought half so base as the malice and guile
Of my own sordid passions, or Satan's control.

For years I have borne about hell in my breast;
When I thought of my God it was nothing but gloom;
Day brought me no pleasure, night gave me no rest,
There was still the grim shadow of horrible doom.

It seemed as if nothing less likely could be
Than that light should break in on a dungeon so deep;
To create a new world were less hard than to free
The slave from his bondage, the soul from its sleep.

But the word had gone forth, and said, Let there be light,
And it flashed through my soul like a sharp passing smart;
One look to my Saviour, and all the dark night,
Like a dream scarce remembered, was gone from my heart.

I cried out for mercy, and fell on my knees,
And confessed, while my heart with keen sorrow was wrung;
'Twas the labor of minutes, and years of disease
Fell as fast from my soul as the words from my tongue.

And now, blest be God and the sweet Lord who died!
No deer on the mountain, no bird in the sky
No bright wave that leaps on the dark bounding tide,
Is a creature so free or so happy as I.

All hail, then, all hail, to the dear Precious Blood,
That hath worked these sweet wonders of mercy in me;
May each day countless numbers throng down to its flood,
And God have His glory, and sinners go free.

—FREDERICK WILLIAM FABER, 1814-1863

A SOUL IN ITS EARLIEST LOVE

O how happy are they
Who their Saviour obey,
And have laid up their treasure above;
Tongue can never express
The sweet comfort and peace
Of a soul in its earliest love.

That sweet comfort was mine,
When the favor divine
I received through the blood of the Lamb;
When my heart first believed,
What a joy I received—
What a heaven in Jesus' Name!

'Twas a heaven below
My Redeemer to know,
And the angels could do nothing more
Than to fall at His feet,
And the story repeat,
And the Lover of sinners adore.

Jesus all the day long
Was my joy and my song:
O that all His salvation might see;
He hath loved me, I cried,
He hath suffered and died,
To redeem even rebels like me.

O the rapturous height
Of that holy delight
Which I felt in the life-giving blood;
Of my Saviour possessed,
I was perfectly blessed
As if filled with the fulness of God.

—*CHARLES WESLEY, 1707-1788*

Yearning for Purity of Heart

I THIRST, THOU WOUNDED LAMB OF GOD

I thirst, Thou wounded Lamb of God,
To wash me in Thy cleansing blood;
To dwell within Thy wounds; then pain
Is sweet, and life or death is gain.

Take my poor heart, and let it be
Forever closed to all but Thee:
Seal Thou my breast, and let me wear
That pledge of love forever there.

How blest are they who still abide
Close shelter'd in Thy bleeding side!
Who thence their life and strength derive,
And by Thee move, and in Thee live.

What are our works but sin and death,
Till Thou thy quick'ning Spirit breathe?
Thou giv'st the power thy grace to move;
O wondrous grace! O boundless love!

How can it be, Thou heavenly King,
That Thou shouldst us to glory bring;
Make slaves the partners of thy throne,
Deck'd with a never-fading crown?

Hence our hearts melt, our eyes o'erflow,
Our words are lost, nor will we know,
Nor will we think of aught beside, —
My Lord, my Love is crucified.

—Attributed to JOHN WESLEY, 1703-1791

PRAYER FOR PURITY

O Thou, to whose all-searching sight
The darkness shineth as the light,
Search, prove my heart; it pants for Thee;
O burst these bonds, and set it free!

Wash out its stains, refine its dross,
Nail my affections to the Cross;
Hallow each thought; let all within
Be clean, as Thou, my Lord, art clean!

If in this darksome wild I stray,
Be Thou my Light, be Thou my Way;
No foes, no violence I fear,
No fraud, while Thou, my God, art near.

When rising floods my soul o'erflow,
When sinks my heart in waves of woe,
Jesus, Thy timely aid impart,
And raise my head, and cheer my heart.

Saviour, where'er Thy steps I see,
Dauntless, untired, I follow Thee;
O let Thy hand support me still,
And lead me to Thy holy hill!

If rough and thorny be the way,
My strength proportion to my day;
Till toil, and grief, and pain shall cease,
Where all is calm, and joy, and peace.

—*NICOLAUS LUDWIG VON ZINZENDORF, 1700-1760*
Tr. JOHN WESLEY, 1703-1791

JESUS, THINE ALL-VICTORIOUS LOVE

Jesus, thine all-victorious love
Shed in my heart abroad:
Then shall my feet no longer rove,
Rooted and fix'd in God.

O that in me the sacred fire
Might now begin to glow;
Burn up the dross of base desire,
And make the mountains flow.

O that it now from heaven might fall,
And all my sins consume:
Come, Holy Ghost, for Thee I call;
Spirit of burning, come.

Refining fire, go through my heart;
Illuminate my soul;
Scatter Thy life through every part,
And sanctify the whole.

My steadfast soul, from falling free,
Shall then no longer move;
While Christ is all the world to me,
And all my heart is love.

—*CHARLES WESLEY, 1707-1788*

SELF-LOVE

Oh I could go through all life's troubles singing,
Turning earth's night to day,
If self were not so fast around me, clinging
To all I do or say.

My very thoughts are selfish, always building
Mean castles in the air;
I use my love of others for a gilding
To make myself look fair.

I fancy all the world engrossed with judging
My merit or my blame;
Its warmest praise seems an ungracious grudging
Of praise which I might claim.

In youth or age, by city, wood, or mountain,
Self is forgotten never;
Where'er we tread, it gushes like a fountain,
And its waters flow for ever.

Alas! no speed in life can snatch us wholly
Out of self's hateful sight;
And it keeps step, whene'er we travel slowly,
And sleeps with us at night.

No grief's sharp knife, no pain's most cruel sawing
Self and the soul can sever:
The surface, that in joy sometimes seems thawing,
Soon freezes worse than ever.

Thus we are never men, self's wretched swathing
Not letting virtue swell;
Thus is our whole life numbed, for ever bathing
Within this frozen well.

O miserable omnipresence, stretching
Over all time and space,
How have I run from thee, yet found thee reaching
The goal in every race.

Inevitable self! vile imitation
Of universal light, —
Within our hearts a dreadful usurpation
Of God's exclusive right!

The opiate balms of grace may haply still thee,
Deep in my nature lying;
For I may hardly hope, alas! to kill thee,
Save by the act of dying.

O Lord! that I could waste my life for others,
With no ends of my own,
That I could pour myself into my brothers,
And live for them alone!

Such was the life Thou livedst; self-abjuring,
Thine own pains never easing,
Our burdens bearing, our just doom enduring,
A life without self-pleasing!

—FREDERICK WILLIAM FABER, 1814-1863

Aspirations After God

AS PANTS THE HART

As pants the hart for cooling streams,
When heated in the chase;
So longs my soul, O God, for Thee,
And Thy refreshing grace.

For Thee, my God, the living God,
My thirsty soul doth pine;
Oh, when shall I behold Thy face,
Thou Majesty divine?

Why restless, why cast down, my soul?
Trust God; who will employ
His aid for thee, and change these sighs
To thankful hymns of joy.

God of my strength, how long shall I,
Like one forgotten, mourn;
Forlorn, forsaken, and exposed
To my oppressor's scorn?

I sigh to think of happier days,
When Thou, O Lord! wast nigh;
When every heart was tuned to praise,
And none more blessed than I.

Why restless, why cast down, my soul?
Hope still; and thou shalt sing
The praise of Him who is Thy God,
Thy health's eternal spring.

—NAHUM TATE, 1652-1715
—NICHOLAS BRADY, 1659-1726
Psalm 42 paraphrase

THE WAY OF PERFECTION

Oh how the thought of God attracts
And draws the heart from earth,
And sickens it of passing shows
And dissipating mirth!

'Tis not enough to save our souls,
To shun the eternal fires;
The thought of God will rouse the heart
To more sublime desires.

God only is the creature's home,
Though rough and straight the road;
Yet nothing less can satisfy
The love that longs for God.

Oh utter but the Name of God
Down in your heart of hearts,
And see how from the world at once
All tempting light departs.

A trusting heart, a yearning eye,
Can win their way above;
If mountains can be moved by faith,
Is there less power in love?

How little of that road, my soul!
How little hast thou gone!
Take heart, and let the thought of God
Allure thee further on.

The freedom from all wilful sin,
The Christian's daily task, —
Oh these are graces far below
What longing love would ask!

Dole not thy duties out to God,
But let thy hand be free:
Look long at Jesus; His sweet Blood,
How was it dealt to thee?

The perfect way is hard to flesh;
It is not hard to love;
If thou wert sick for want of God,
How swiftly wouldst thou move!

Then keep thy conscience sensitive;
No inward token miss:
And go where grace entices thee; —
Perfection lies in this.

Be docile to thine unseen Guide,
Love Him as He loves thee;
Time and obedience are enough,
And thou a saint shall be.

—FREDERICK WILLIAM FABER, 1814-1863

THOU SHEPHERD OF ISRAEL, AND MINE

Thou Shepherd of Israel, and mine,
The joy and desire of my heart,
For closer communion I pine;
I long to reside where Thou art:
The pasture I languish to find,
Where all, who their Shepherd obey,
Are fed, on Thy bosom reclined,
And screen'd from the heat of the day.

'Tis there, with the lambs of Thy flock,
There only, I covet to rest;
To lie at the foot of the rock,
Or rise to be hid in Thy breast:
'Tis there I would always abide,
And never a moment depart, —
Conceal'd in the cleft of Thy side,
Eternally held in Thy heart.

—*CHARLES WESLEY, 1707-1788*

THE FERVOR OF HOLY DESIRE

Still, still, without ceasing,
I feel it increasing,
This fervor of holy desire;
And often exclaim,
Let me die in the flame
Of a love that can never expire!

Had I words to explain,
What she must sustain,
Who dies to the world and its ways;
How joy and affright,
Distress and delight,
Alternately checker her days;

Thou, sweetly severe!
I would make thee appear,
In all thou art pleas'd to award,
Not more in the sweet,
Than the bitter I meet,
My tender and merciful Lord.

This Faith, in the dark
Pursuing its mark,
Through many sharp trials of Love,
Is the sorrowful waste,
That is to be pass'd,
In the way to the Canaan above.

—*JEANNE MARIE DE LA MOTTE-GUYON, 1648-1717*

Tr. Unknown

DESIRE OF GOD

Oh for freedom, for freedom in worshipping God,
For the mountain-top feeling of generous souls,
For the health, for the air, of the hearts deep and broad,
Where grace not in rills but in cataracts rolls!

Most good is the brisk wholesome service of fear,
And the calm wise obedience of conscience is sweet;
And good are all worships, all loyalties dear,
All promptitudes fitting, all services meet.

But none honours God like the thirst of desire,
Nor possesses the heart so completely with Him;
For it burns the world out with the swift ease of fire,
And fills life with good works till it runs o'er the brim.

Then pray for desire, for love's wistfullest yearning,
For the beautiful pining of holy desire;
Yes, pray for a soul that is ceaselessly burning
With the soft fragrant flames of this thrice happy fire.

For the heart only dwells, truly dwells with its treasure,
And the languor of love captive hearts can unfetter;
And they who love God cannot love Him by measure,
For their love is but hunger to love Him still better.

Is it hard to serve God, timid soul? Hast thou found
Gloomy forests, dark glens, mountain-tops on thy way?
All the hard would be easy, all the tangles unwound,
Wouldst thou only desire, as well as obey.

For the lack of desire is the ill of all ills;
Many thousands through it the dark pathway have trod,
The balsam, the wine of predestinate wills
Is a jubilant pining and longing for God.

'Tis a fire that will burn what thou canst not pass over;
'Tis a lightning that breaks away all bars to love;
'Tis a sunbeam the secrets of God to discover;
'Tis the wing David prayed for, the wing of the Dove.

I have seen living men—and their good angels know
How they failed and fell short through the want of desire:
Souls once almost saints have descended so low,
'Twill be much if their wings bear them over the fire.

I have seen dying men not so grand in their dying
As our love would have wished,—and through lack of desire:
Oh that we may die languishing, burning, and sighing;
For God's last grace and best is to die all on fire.

'Tis a great gift of God to live after our Lord,
Yet the old Hebrew times they were ages of fire.
When fainting souls fed on each dim figured word,
And God called men He loved most—the Men of Desire.

Oh then wish more for God, burn more with desire,
Covet more the dear sight of his marvellous Face;
Pray louder, pray longer, for the sweet gift of fire
To come down on thy heart with its whirlwinds of grace.

Yes, pine for thy God, fainting soul! Ever pine;
Oh languish mid all that life brings thee of mirth;
Famished, thirsty, and restless, —let such life be thine,—
For what sight is to heaven, desire is to earth.

God loves to be longed for, He loves to be sought,
For He sought us Himself with such longing and love:
He died for desire of us, marvellous thought!
And He yearns for us now to be with Him above.

—FREDERICK WILLIAM FABER, 1814-1863

SATISFIED

Draw me to Thee, till far within Thy rest,
In stillness of Thy peace, Thy voice I hear—
For ever quieted upon Thy breast,
So loved, so near.

By mystery of Thy touch my spirit thrilled,
O Magnet all Divine;
The hunger of my soul for ever stilled,
For Thou art mine.

For me, O Lord, the world is all too small,
For I have seen Thy face,
Where Thine eternal love irradiates all
Within Thy secret place.
And therefore from all others, from all else,
Draw Thou my soul to Thee . . .
. . . Yea—Thou hast broken the enchanter's spells,
And I am free.

Now in the haven of untroubled rest
I land at last,
The hunger, and the thirst, and weary quest
For ever past.
There, Lord, to lose, in bliss of Thine embrace
The recreant will;
There, in the radiance of Thy blessed Face,
Be hushed and still;
There, speechless at Thy pierced Feet
See none and nought beside,
And know but this—that Thou art sweet,
That I am satisfied.

—GERHARD TERSTEEGEN, 1697-1769
Tr. Unknown

DELIGHTING IN GOD'S PRESENCE

GOD IS PRESENT EVERYWHERE

They who seek the throne of grace
Find that throne in every place;
If we live a life of prayer,
God is present everywhere.

In our sickness and our health,
In our want, or in our wealth,
If we look to God in prayer,
God is present everywhere.

When our earthly comforts fail,
When the woes of life prevail,
'Tis the time for earnest prayer;
God is present everywhere.

Then, my soul, in every strait,
To thy Father come, and wait;
He will answer every prayer:
God is present everywhere.

—OLIVER HOLDEN, 1765-1844

THE ROYAL PRIESTHOOD

The race of God's anointed priests
Shall never pass away;
Before His glorious face they stand,
And serve Him night and day.
Though reason raves, and unbelief
Flows on, a mighty flood,
There are, and shall be till the end,
The hidden priests of God.

His chosen souls, their earthly dross
Consumed in sacred fire,
To God's own heart their hearts ascend
In flame of deep desire;
The incense of their worship fills
His Temple's holiest place;
Their song with wonder fills the Heavens,
The glad new song of grace.

—*GERHARD TERSTEEGEN, 1697-1769*
Tr. Unknown

GOD REVEALS HIS PRESENCE

God reveals His presence:
Let us now adore Him,
And with awe appear before Him.
God is in His temple:
All within keep silence,
Prostrate lie with deepest reverence.
Him alone
God we own,
Him our God and Saviour:
Praise His Name for ever!

God reveals His presence:
Hear the harps resounding;
See the crowds the throne surrounding;
"Holy, holy, holy!"

Hear the hymn ascending,
Angels, saints, their voices blending.
Bow Thine ear
To us here;
Hearken, O Lord Jesus,
To our meaner praises.

O Thou Fount of blessing
Purify my spirit,
Trusting only in Thy merit:
Like the holy angels
Who behold Thy glory,
May I ceaselessly adore Thee.
Let Thy will
Ever still
Rule Thy Church terrestrial,
As the hosts celestial.

—GERHARD TERSTEEGEN, 1697-1769
Composite translation

WITHIN THE HOLY PLACE

His priest am I, before Him day and night,
Within His Holy Place;
And death, and life, and all things dark and bright,
I spread before His Face.
Rejoicing with His joy, yet ever still,
For silence is my song;
My work to bend beneath His blessed will,
All day, and all night long—
For ever holding with Him converse sweet,
Yet speechless, for my gladness is complete.

—GERHARD TERSTEEGEN, 1697-1769
Tr. Unknown

LO, GOD IS HERE!

Lo, God is here! let us adore,
And own how dreadful is this place;
Let all within us feel His power,
And silent bow before His face;
Who know His power, His grace who prove,
Serve Him with awe, with reverence love.

Lo, God is here! Him day and night
United choirs of angels sing;
To Him, enthroned above all height,
Heaven's host their noblest praises bring;
Disdain not, Lord, our meaner song,
Who praise Thee with a stammering tongue.

Being of beings, may our praise
Thy courts with grateful fragrance fill;
Still may we stand before Thy face,
Still hear and do Thy sovereign will;
To Thee may all our thoughts arise,
Ceaseless, accepted sacrifice.

—GERHARD TERSTEEGEN, 1697-1769
Tr. JOHN WESLEY, 1703-1791

ALLURED INTO THE DESERT

Allured into the desert,
With God alone, apart,
There spirit meeteth spirit,
There speaketh heart to heart.
Far, far on that untrodden shore,
God's secret place I find;
Alone I pass the golden door,
The dearest left behind.

There God and I—none other;
Oh far from men to be!
Nay, midst the crowd and tumult,

Still, Lord, alone with Thee.
Still folded close upon Thy breast,
In field, and mart, and street,
Untroubled in that perfect rest,
That isolation sweet.

O God, Thou art far other
Than men have dreamed and taught,
Unspoken in all language,
Unpictured in all thought.
Thou God art God—he only learns
What that great Name must be,
Whose raptured heart within him burns,
Because he walks with Thee.

Stilled by that wondrous Presence,
That tenderest embrace,
The years of longing over,
Do we behold Thy Face;
We seek no more than Thou hast given,
We ask no vision fair,
Thy precious Blood has opened Heaven,
And we have found Thee there.

O weary souls, draw near Him;
To you I can but bring
One drop of that great ocean,
One blossom of that spring;
Sealed with His kiss, my lips are dumb,
My soul with awe is still;
Let him that is athirst but come,
And freely drink his fill.

—GERHARD TERSTEEGEN, 1697-1769
Tr. Unknown

The Raptures of Divine Love

O LOVE DIVINE!

O Love Divine! that stoop'st to share
Our sharpest pang, our bitterest tear,
On Thee we cast each earth-born care,
We smile at pain while Thou art near.

Though long the weary way we tread,
And sorrow crown each lingering year,
No path we shun, no darkness dread,
Our hearts still whispering, "Thou art near."

When drooping pleasure turns to grief,
And trembling faith is changed to fear,
The murmuring wind, the quivering leaf,
Shall softly tell us Thou art near.

On Thee we cast our burdening woe,
O Love Divine, for ever dear;
Content to suffer while we know,
Living or dying, Thou art near!

—OLIVER WENDELL HOLMES, 1809-1894

I LOVE MY GOD

I love my God, but with no love of mine,
For I have none to give;
I love thee, Lord; but all the love is Thine,
For by Thy life I live.
I am as nothing, and rejoice to be
Emptied, and lost, and swallowed up in Thee.

Thou, Lord, alone, art all Thy children need,
And there is none beside;
From Thee the streams of blessedness proceed
In Thee the blest abide, —
Fountain of life, and all-abounding grace,
Our source, our center, and our dwelling-place.

—*JEANNE MARIE DE LA MOTTE-GUYON, 1648-1717*
Tr. Unknown

THE ACQUIESCENCE OF PURE LOVE

Love! if thy destined sacrifice am I,
Come, slay thy victim, and prepare Thy fires;
Plunged in Thy depths of mercy, let me die
The death which every soul that lives desires.

I watch my hours, and see them fleet away;
The time is long that I have languished here;
Yet all my thoughts Thy purposes obey,
With no reluctance, cheerful and sincere.

To me 'tis equal, whether Love ordain
My life or death, appoint me pain or ease;
My soul perceives no real ill in pain;
In ease or health no real good she sees.

One good she covets, and that good alone,
To choose Thy will, from selfish bias free;
And to prefer a cottage to a throne,
And grief to comfort, if it pleases Thee.

That we should bear the cross is Thy command,
Die to the world, and live to self no more;
Suffer, unmoved, beneath the rudest hand;
When shipwrecked pleased as when upon the shore.

—JEANNE MARIE DE LA MOTTE-GUYON, 1648-1717
Tr. Unknown

JESUS, THY BOUNDLESS LOVE TO ME

Jesus, Thy boundless love to me
No thought can reach, no tongue declare;
O knit my thankful heart to Thee,
And reign without a rival there:
Thine wholly, Thine alone I am:
Be Thou alone my constant flame.

O grant that nothing in my soul
May dwell, but Thy pure love alone;
O may Thy love possess me whole,
My joy, my treasure, and my crown:
Strange fires far from my soul remove;
May every act, word, thought, be love.

O Love, how cheering is Thy ray;
All pain before Thy presence flies;
Care, anguish, sorrow, melt away,
Where'er Thy healing beams arise;
O Jesus, nothing may I see,
Nothing desire, or seek, but Thee.

In suffering, be Thy love my peace;
In weakness, be Thy love my power;
And, when the storms of life shall cease,
Jesus, in that important hour,
In death, as life, be Thou my guide,
And save me, who for me hast died.

—PAUL GERHARDT, 1607-1676
Tr. John Wesley, 1703-1791

O LOVE DIVINE!

O Love divine, how sweet Thou art!
When shall I find my willing heart
All taken up by Thee?
I thirst, I faint, I die to prove
The greatness of redeeming love,—
The love of Christ to me.

Stronger His love than death or hell;
Its riches are unsearchable;
The first-born sons of light
Desire in vain its depths to see;
They cannot reach the mystery,
The length, the breadth, the height.

God only knows the love of God;
O that it now were shed abroad
In this poor stony heart:
For love I sigh, for love I pine;
This only portion, Lord, be mine;
Be mine this better part.

O that I could forever sit
With Mary at the Master's feet!
Be this my happy choice;
My only care, delight, and bliss,
My joy, my heaven on earth, be this,
To hear the Bridegroom's voice.

O that I could, with favor'd John,
Recline my weary head upon
The dear Redeemer's breast:
From care, and sin, and sorrow free,
Give me, O Lord, to find in Thee
My everlasting rest.

—*CHARLES WESLEY, 1707-1788*

THE HIDDEN LOVE OF GOD

Thou hidden Love of God, whose height,
Whose depth unfathomed, no man knows,
I see from far Thy beauteous light,
Inly I sigh for Thy repose;
My heart is pained, nor can it be
At rest till it finds rest in Thee.

Thy secret voice invites me still
The sweetness of Thy yoke to prove;
And fain I would; but, though my will
Seem fixed, yet wide my passions rove.
Yet hindrances strew all the way;
I aim at Thee, yet from Thee stray.

'Tis mercy all, that Thou hast brought
My mind to seek her peace in Thee;
Yet, while I seek but find Thee not,
No peace my wandering soul shall see.
O when shall all my wanderings end,
And all my steps to Thee-ward tend?

Is there a thing beneath the sun
That strives with Thee my heart to share?
Ah! tear it thence, and reign alone,
The Lord of every motion there;
Then shall my heart from earth be free,
When it hath found repose in Thee.

—GERHARD TERSTEEGEN, 1697-1769
Tr. John Wesley, 1703-1791

LOVE'S IMMENSITY

O past and gone!
How great is God! how small am I!
A mote in the illimitable sky,
Amidst the glory deep, and wide, and high
Of Heaven's unclouded sun.
There to forget myself for evermore;
Lost, swallowed up in Love's immensity,
The sea that knows no sounding and no shore,
God only there, not I.

More near than I unto myself can be,
Art Thou to me;
So have I lost myself in finding Thee,
Have lost myself for ever, O my Sun!
The boundless Heaven of Thine eternal love
Around me, and beneath me, and above;
In glory of that golden day
The former things are passed away—
I, past and gone.

—GERHARD TERSTEEGEN, 1697-1769

The Rest of Faith

ALL MUST BE WELL

Through the love of God our Saviour,
All will be well;
Free and changeless is His favor,
All, all is well;
Precious is the blood that heard us,
Perfect is the grace that seed us,
Strong the hand stretch'd out to shield us,
All must be well.

Though we pass through tribulation,
All will be well;
Ours is such a full salvation,
All, all is well;
Happy, still in God confiding,
Fruitful, if in Christ abiding
Holy, through the Spirit's guiding,
All must be well.

We expect a bright tomorrow,
All will be well;
Faith can sing, through days of sorrow,
All, all is well;
On our Father's love relying,
Jesus ev'ry need supplying,
Or in living or in dying,
All must be well.

—*MARY BOWLEY PETERS, 1813-1856*

CONFIDENCE

If thou but suffer God to guide thee,
And hope in Him through all thy ways,
He'll give thee strength, whate'er betide thee,
And bear thee through the evil days;
Who trusts in God's unchanging love
Builds on the rock that nought can move.

What can these anxious cares avail thee,
These never-ceasing moans and sighs?
What can it help if thou bewail thee
O'er each dark moment as it flies?
Our cross and trials do but press
The heavier for our bitterness.

Only be still, and wait His leisure
In cheerful hope, with heart content
To take whate'er thy Father's pleasure
And all-discerning love hath sent;
Nor doubt our inmost wants are known
To Him who chose us for His own.

Sing, pray, and keep His ways unswerving;
So do thine own part faithfully,
And trust His word,—though undeserving,
Thou yet shalt find it true for thee;
God never yet forsook at need
The soul that trusted Him indeed.

—GEORGE C. NEUMARK, 1621-1681
Tr. Catherine Winkworth, 1829-1878

SOMETIMES A LIGHT SURPRISES

Sometimes a light surprises
The Christian while he sings;
It is the Lord, who rises
With healing in His wings:
When comforts are declining,
He grants the soul again
A season of clear shining,
To cheer it after rain.

In holy contemplation,
We sweetly then pursue
The theme of God's salvation,
And find it ever new:
Set free from present sorrow,
We cheerfully can say,
"E'en let the unknown morrow
Bring with it what it may."

It can bring with it nothing,
But He will bear us through;
Who gives the lilies clothing,
Will clothe His people too:
Beneath the spreading heavens,
No creature but is fed;
And He who feeds the ravens
Will give His children bread.

—*WILLIAM COWPER, 1731-1800*

THE BLESSED JOURNEY

Let Him lead thee blindfold onwards,
Love needs not to know;
Children whom the Father leadeth
Ask not where they go.
Though the path be all unknown,
Over moors and mountains lone.

Give no ear to reason's questions;
Let the blind man hold
That the sun is but a fable
Men believed of old.
At the breast the babe will grow;
Whence the milk he need not know.

—GERHARD TERSTEEGEN, 1697-1769
Tr. Unknown

JESUS, I AM RESTING, RESTING

Jesus, I am resting, resting
In the joy of what Thou art,
I am finding out the greatness
Of Thy loving heart.
Here I gaze and gaze upon Thee,
As Thy beauty fills my soul,
For by Thy transforming power,
Thou hast made me whole.

O how great Thy loving-kindness,
Vaster, broader than the sea;
O how marvellous Thy goodness
Lavished all on me—
Yes, I rest in Thee, Beloved,
Know what wealth of grace is Thine,
Know Thy certainty of promise
And have made it mine.

Simply trusting Thee, Lord Jesus,
I behold Thee as Thou art,
And Thy love, so pure, so changeless,
Satisfies my heart,
Satisfies its deepest longing,
Meets, supplies my every need,
Compasseth me round with blessings:
Thine is love indeed.

Ever lift Thy face upon me
As I work and wait for Thee;
Resting 'neath Thy smile, Lord Jesus,
Earth's dark shadows flee.
Brightness of my Father's glory,
Sunshine of my Father's face,
Let Thy glory e'er shine on me,
Fill me with Thy grace.

—*JEAN SOPHIA PIGOTT, 19th Century*

RESIGNATION

A little bird I am,
Shut from the fields of air;
And in my cage I sit and sing
To Him who placed me there;
Well pleased a prisoner to be,
Because, my God, it pleases Thee.

Naught have I else to do;
I sing the whole day long;
And He whom most I love to please
Doth listen to my song;
He caught and bound my wandering wing,
But still He bends to hear me sing.

Thou hast an ear to hear,
A heart to love and bless;
And though my notes were e'er so rude,
Thou wouldst not hear the less;
Because Thou knowest, as they fall,
That love, sweet love, inspires them all.

My cage confines me round;
Abroad I cannot fly;
But though my wing is closely bound,
My heart's at liberty.
My prison walls cannot control
The flight, the freedom, of the soul.

O, it is good to soar
These bolts and bars above,
To Him whose purpose I adore,
Whose providence I love;
And in Thy mighty will to find
The joy, the freedom, of the mind.

—*JEANNE MARIE DE LA MOTTE-GUYON, 1648-1717*
Tr. Unknown

IN HEAVENLY LOVE ABIDING

In heavenly love abiding,
No change my heart shall fear;
And safe is such confiding,
For nothing changes here:
The storm may roar without me,
My heart may low be laid;
But God is round about me,
And can I be dismayed?

Wherever He may guide me,
No want shall turn me back;
My Shepherd is beside me,
And nothing can I lack.
His wisdom ever waketh,
His sight is never dim:
He knows the way He taketh,
And I will walk with Him.

Green pastures are before me,
Which yet I have not seen;
Bright skies will soon be o'er me,
Where the dark clouds have been.
My hope I cannot measure:
My path to life is free:
My Saviour has my treasure,
And He will walk with me.

—*ANNA LAETITIA WARING, 1820-1910*

THE REMEMBRANCE OF MERCY

Why art thou sorrowful, servant of God?
And what is this dullness that hangs o'er thee now?
Sing the praises of Jesus, and sing them aloud,
And the song shall dispel the dark cloud from thy brow.

For is there a thought in the wide world so sweet,
As that God has so cared for us, bad as we are,
That He thinks of us, plans for us, stoops to entreat,
And follows us, wander we ever so far?

Then how can the heart e'er be drooping or sad,
Which God hath once touched with the light of His grace?
Can the child have a doubt who but lately hath laid
Himself to repose in his father's embrace?

And is it not wonderful, servant of God!
That He should have honoured us so with His love,
That the sorrows of life should but shorten the road
Which leads to Himself and the mansion above?

Oh then when the spirit of darkness comes down
With clouds and uncertainties into thy heart,
One look to thy Saviour, one thought of thy crown,
And the tempest is over, the shadows depart.

That God hath once whispered a word in thine ear,
Or sent thee from heaven one sorrow for sin,
Is enough for a life both to banish all fear,
And to turn into peace all the troubles within.

The schoolmen can teach thee far less about heaven,
Of the height of God's power, or the depth of His love,
Than the fire in thy heart when thy sin was forgiven,
Or the light that one mercy brings down from above.

Then why dost thou weep so? For see how time flies,
The time that for loving and praising was given!
Away with thee, child, then, and hide thy red eyes

In the lap, the kind lap, of thy Father in heaven.

—FREDERICK WILLIAM FABER, 1814-1863

The Spiritual Warfare

DISTRACTIONS IN PRAYER

Ah dearest Lord! I cannot pray,
My fancy is not free;
Unmannerly distractions come,
And force my thoughts from Thee.

The world that looks so dull all day
Glows bright on me at prayer,
And plans that ask no thought but then
Wake up and meet me there.

All nature one full fountain seems
Of dreamy sight and sound,
Which, when I kneel, breaks up its deeps,
And makes a deluge round.

Old voices murmur in my ear,
New hopes start to life,
And past and future gaily blend
In one bewitching strife.

My very flesh has restless fits;
My changeful limbs conspire
With all these phantoms of the mind
My inner self to tire.

I cannot pray; yet, Lord! Thou knowst
The pain it is to me
To have my vainly struggling thoughts
Thus torn away from Thee.

Sweet Jesus! teach me how to prize
These tedious hours when I,
Foolish and mute before Thy Face,
In helpless worship lie.

Prayer was not meant for luxury,
Or selfish pastime sweet;
It is the prostrate creature's place
At his Creator's Feet.

Had I, dear Lord! no pleasure found
But in the thought of Thee,
Prayer would have come unsought, and been
A truer liberty.

Yet Thou art oft most present, Lord!
In weak distracted prayer:
A sinner out of heart with self
Most often finds Thee there.

For prayer that humbles sets the soul
From all illusions free,
And teaches it how utterly,
Dear Lord! it hangs on Thee.

The heart, that on self-sacrifice
Is covetously bent,
Will bless Thy chastening hand that makes
Its prayer its punishment.

My Saviour! why should I complain
And why fear aught but sin?
Distractions are but outward things;
Thy peace dwells far within.

These surface-troubles come and go,
Like rufflings of the sea;
The deeper depth is out of reach
To all, my God, but Thee.

—FREDERIC WILLIAM FABER, 1814-1863

THE BENEFITS OF SUFFERING

By sufferings only can we know
The nature of the life we live;
The temper of our souls they show,
How true, how pure, the love we give.
To leave my love in doubt would be
No less disgrace than misery!

I welcome, then, with heart sincere,
The cross my Saviour bids me take;
No load, no trial, is severe,
That's borne or suffered for His sake:
And thus my sorrow shall proclaim
A love that's worthy of the name.

—JEANNE MARIE DE LA MOTTE-GUYON, 1648-1717
Tr. Unknown

SORROW AND LOVE

Self-love no grace in sorrow sees,
Consults her own peculiar ease,
'Tis all the bliss she knows;
But nobler aims true Love employ,
In self-denial is her joy,
In suffering her repose.

Sorrow and Love go side by side;
Nor height nor depth can e'er divide
Their heaven-appointed bands;
Those dear associates still are one,
Nor, till the race of life is run,
Disjoin their wedded hands.

Thy choice and mine shall be the same,
Inspirer of that holy flame,
Which must forever blaze!
To take the cross and follow Thee,
Where love and duty lead, shall be
My portion and my praise.

—JEANNE MARIE DE LA MOTTE-GUYON, 1648-1717
Tr. Unknown

Victory Through Praise

COME, O MY SOUL

Come, O my soul, in sacred lays,
Attempt thy great Creator's praise:
But, oh, what tongue can speak His fame!
What mortal verse can reach the theme!

Enthroned amid the radiant spheres,
He glory like a garment wears;
To form a robe of light divine,
Ten thousand suns around Him shine.

In all our Maker's grand designs,
Omnipotence, with wisdom, shines;
His works, through all this wondrous frame,
Declare the glory of His Name.

Raised on devotion's lofty wing,
Do thou, my soul, His glories sing;
And let His praise employ thy tongue,
Till listening worlds shall join the song!

—THOMAS BLACKLOCK, 18th Century

BLESS, O MY SOUL, THE LIVING GOD

Bless, O my soul, the living God,
Call home thy thoughts that rove abroad;
Let all the pow'rs within me join
In work and worship so divine.

Bless, O my soul, the God of grace;
His favors claim thy highest praise;
Why should the wonders He hath wrought
Be lost in silence, and forgot?

'Tis He, my soul, that sent His Son
To die for crimes which thou hast done;
He owns the ransom, and forgives
The hourly follies of our lives.

Let the whole earth His power confess,
Let the whole earth adore His grace;
The Gentile with the Jew shall join
In work and worship so divine.

—ISAAC WATTS, 1674-1748
After Psalm 103

I'LL PRAISE MY MAKER

I'll praise my Maker while I've breath,
And when my voice is lost in death,
Praise shall employ my nobler powers;
My days of praise shall ne'er be past,
While life, and thought, and being last,
Or immortality endures.

Happy the man whose hopes rely
On Israel's God; He made the sky,
And earth, and seas, with all their train;
His truth for ever stands secure,
He saves the opprest, He feeds the poor,
And none shall find His promise vain.

The Lord pours eyesight on the blind;
The Lord supports the fainting mind;
He sends the labouring conscience peace;
He helps the stranger in distress,
The widow and the fatherless,
And grants the prisoner sweet release.

I'll praise Him while He lends me breath,
And when my voice is lost in death,
Praise shall employ my nobler powers;
My days of praise shall ne'er be past,
While life, and thought, and being last,
Or immortality endures.

—ISSAC WATTS, 1674-1748
Al. John Wesley, 1703-1791

I SING TH' ALMIGHTY POWER OF GOD

I sing th' almighty power of God,
That made the mountains rise,
That spread the flowing seas abroad,
And built the lofty skies.

I sing the wisdom that ordained
The sun to rule the day;
The moon shines full at His command,
And all the stars obey.

I sing the goodness of the Lord,
That filled the earth with food;
He formed the creatures with His word,
And then pronounced them good.

Lord! how Thy wonders are displayed
Where'er I turn mine eye!
If I survey the ground I tread,
Or gaze upon the sky!

There's not a plant or flower below
But makes Thy glories known;
And clouds arise, and tempests blow,
By order from Thy throne.

Creatures that borrow life from Thee
Are subject to Thy care;
There's not a place where we can flee
But God is present there.

—ISAAC WATTS, 1674-1748

NOW THANK WE ALL OUR GOD

Now thank we all our God,
With heart, and hands, and voices,
Who wondrous things hath done,
In whom His world rejoices;
Who from our mother's arms
Hath blessed us on our way
With countless gifts of love,
And still is ours today.

O may this bounteous God
Through all our life be near us,
With ever joyful hearts
And blessed peace to cheer us;
And keep us in His grace,
And guide us when perplexed,
And free us from all ills
In this world and the next.

All praise and thanks to God
The Father now be given,
The Son, and Him who reigns
With them in highest heaven,
The one eternal God,
Whom earth and heaven adore;
For thus it was, is now,
And shall be evermore.

—MARTIN RINCKART, 1586-1649
Tr. Catharine Winkworth, 1829-1878

TE DEUM LAUDAMUS

We praise Thee, O God,
we acknowledge Thee to be the Lord.
All the earth doth worship Thee, the Father everlasting.
To Thee all angels cry aloud, the heavens and all the powers therein;
To Thee Cherubim and Seraphim continually do cry,
Holy, holy, holy, Lord God of Sabaoth:
Heaven and earth are full of the majesty of Thy glory.
The glorious company of the Apostles praise Thee.
The goodly fellowship of the Prophets praise Thee.
The noble army of Martyrs praise Thee.
The holy Church throughout all the world doth acknowledge Thee,
The Father of an infinite Majesty;
Thine adorable, true and only Son;
Also the Holy Ghost, the Comforter.

Thou art the King of Glory, O Christ;
Thou art the everlasting Son of the Father.
When Thou tookest upon Thee to deliver man
Thou didst humble Thyself to be born of a virgin.
When Thou hadst overcome the sharpness of death
Thou didst open the kingdom of heaven to all believers.
Thou sittest at the right hand of God in the glory of the Father.
We believe that Thou shalt come to be our Judge.
We therefore pray Thee help Thy servants whom
Thou hast redeemed with Thy precious blood.
Make them to be numbered with Thy saints in glory everlasting.

O Lord, save Thy people, and bless Thine heritage.
Govern them, and lift them up forever.
Day by day we magnify Thee,
And we worship Thy Name forever, world without end.
Vouchsafe, O Lord, to keep us this day without sin.
O Lord, have mercy upon us, have mercy upon us.
O Lord, let Thy mercy be upon us, as our trust is in Thee.
O Lord, in Thee have I trusted, let me never be confounded.

THE PRAYER OF QUIET

THE SPIRIT OF PRAYER

The prayers I make will then be sweet indeed
If Thou the Spirit give by which I pray:
My unassisted heart is barren clay,
That of its native self can nothing feed:
Of good and pious works Thou art the seed,
That quickens only where Thou say'st it may:
Unless Thou show to us Thine own true way
No man can find it: Father! Thou must lead.
Do Thou, then, breathe those thoughts into my mind
By which such virtue may in me be bred
That in Thy holy footsteps I may tread;
The fetters of my tongue do Thou unbind,
That I may have the power to sing of Thee,
And sound Thy praises everlastingly.

—FROM THE ITALIAN OF MICHAEL ANGELO, 1475-1564
Tr. William Wordsworth, 1770-1850

MY GOD! SILENT TO THEE!

As, down in the sunless retreats of the ocean,
Sweet flowers are springing no mortal can see,
So, deep in my heart, the still prayer of devotion,
Unheard by the world, rises, silent, to Thee,
My God! silent, to Thee,—

Pure, warm, silent, to Thee.
As still to the star of its worship, though clouded,
The needle points faithfully o'er the dim sea,
So, dark as I roam, thro' this wintry world shrouded,
The hope of my spirit turns, trembling, to Thee,
My God! trembling, to Thee,—
True, fond, trembling, to Thee.

—THOMAS MOORE, 1719-1852

GOD'S ETERNAL NOW

Stillness midst the ever-changing,
Lord, my rest art Thou;
So for me has dawned the morning,
God's eternal NOW.
Now for me the day unsetting,
Now the song begun;
Now, the deep surpassing glory,
Brighter than the sun.

Hail! all hail! thou peaceful country
Of eternal calm;
Summer land of milk and honey,
Where the streams are balm.
There the Lord my Shepherd leads me,
Wheresoe'er He will;
In the fresh green pastures feeds me,
By the waters still.

Well I know them, those still waters!
Peace and rest at last;
In their depths the quiet heavens
Tell the storms are past,
Nought to mar the picture fair,
Of the glory resting there.

—GERHARD TERSTEEGEN, 1697-1769
Tr. Unknown

MY HEART IS RESTING, O MY GOD

My heart is resting, O my God,
I will give thanks and sing;
My heart is at the secret source
Of every precious thing.
Now the frail vessel Thou hast made
No hand but Thine shall fill;
For the waters of the earth have failed,
And I am thirsty still.

I thirst for springs of heavenly life,
And here all day they rise;
I seek the treasure of Thy love,
And close at hand it lies.
And a new song is in my mouth
To long-loved music set:
"Glory to Thee for all the grace
I have not tasted yet;

"Glory to Thee for strength withheld,
For want and weakness known;
And the fear that sends me to Thy breast
For what is most my own."
I have a heritage of joy
That yet I must not see;
But the hand that bled to make it mine
Is keeping it for me.

My heart is resting, O my God,
My heart is in Thy care;
I hear the voice of joy and health
Resounding everywhere.
"Thou art my portion," saith my soul,
Ten thousand voices say,
And the music of their glad Amen
Will never die away.

—*ANNA LAETITIA WARING, 1820-1910*

HIDDEN IN GOD'S HEART

How good it is, when weaned from all beside,
With God alone the soul is satisfied,
Deep hidden in His heart!
How good it is, redeemed, and washed, and shriven,
To dwell, a cloistered soul, with Christ in heaven,
Joined, never more to part!

How good the heart's still chamber thus to close
On all but God alone—
There in the sweetness of His love repose,
His love unknown!
All else for ever lost—forgotten all
That else can be;
In rapture undisturbed, O Lord, to fall
And worship Thee.

No place, no time, 'neath those eternal skies—
How still, how sweet, and how surpassing fair
That solitude in glades of Paradise,
And, as in olden days, God walking there.
I hear His voice amidst the stillness blest,
And care and fear are past—
I lay me down within His arms to rest
From all my works at last.

How good it is when from the distant land,
From lonely wanderings, and from weary ways,
The soul hath reached at last the golden strand,
The Gates of Praise!
There, where the tide of endless love flows free,
There, in the sweet and glad eternity,
The still, unfading Now.
Ere yet the days and nights of earth are o'er,
Begun the day that is for evermore—
Such rest art Thou!

—*GERHARD TERSTEEGEN, 1697-1769*
Tr. Unknown

THE BLISS OF COMMUNION

THE DISCIPLE TO HIS LORD

Teach me to do the thing that pleaseth Thee;
Thou art my God, in Thee I live and move;
Oh, let Thy loving Spirit lead me forth
Into the land of righteousness and love.

Thy love the law and impulse of my soul,
Thy righteousness its fitness and its plea,
Thy loving Spirit mercy's sweet control
To make me liker, draw me nearer Thee.

My highest hope to be where, Lord, Thou art,
To lose myself in Thee my richest gain,
To do Thy will the habit of my heart,
To grieve the Spirit my severest pain.

Thy smile my sunshine, all my peace from thence,
From self alone what could that peace destroy?
Thy joy my sorrow at the least offence,
My sorrow that I am not more Thy joy.

—JOHN S. B. MONSELL, 1811-1875

JOY IN THE PRESENCE OF JESUS

How tedious and tasteless the hours
When Jesus no longer I see!
Sweet prospects, sweet birds, and sweet flowers,
Have all lost their sweetness to me;-

The midsummer sun shines but dim,
The fields strive in vain to look gay;
But when I am happy in Him,
December's as pleasant as May.

His Name yields the richest perfume,
And sweeter than music His voice;
His presence disperses my gloom,
And makes all within me rejoice;

I should, were He always thus nigh,
Have nothing to wish or to fear;
No mortal so happy as I,
My summer would last all the year.

Content with beholding His face,
My all to His pleasure resign'd,
No changes of season or place
Would make any change in my mind:

While blest with a sense of His love,
A palace a toy would appear;
And prisons would palaces prove,
If Jesus would dwell with me there.

My Lord, if indeed I am Thine,
If Thou art my sun and my song,
Say, why do I languish and pine?
And why are my winters so long?

O drive these dark clouds from my sky;
Thy soul-cheering presence restore;
Or take me to Thee up on high,
Where winter and clouds are no more.

—JOHN NEWTON, 1725-1807

O JESUS, KING MOST WONDERFUL

O Jesus, King most wonderful,
Thou Conqueror renowned,
Thou Sweetness most ineffable,
In whom all joys are found!

When once Thou visitest the heart,
Then truth begins to shine,
Then earthly vanities depart,
Then kindles love divine.

O Jesus, Light of all below!
Thou Fount of life and fire!
Surpassing all the joys we know,
And all we can desire,—

May every heart confess Thy Name,
And ever Thee adore,
And, seeking Thee, itself inflame
To seek Thee more and more.

Thee may our tongues for ever bless,
Thee may we love alone,
And ever in our lives express
The image of Thine own.

—BERNARD OF CLAIRVAUX, 1091-1153
Tr. Edward Caswall, 1814-1878

CHRIST OUR LIGHT

O Christ our Light, Whom even in darkness we
(So we look up) discern and gaze upon,
O Christ, Thou loveliest Light that ever shone,
Thou Light of Light, Fount of all lights that be,
Grant us clear vision of Thy Light to see,
Tho' other lights elude us, or begone
Into the secret of oblivion,
Or gleam in places higher than man's degree.

Who looks on Thee looks full on his desire
Who looks on Thee looks full on Very Love:
Looking, he answers well, "What lack I yet?"
His heat and cold wait not on earthly fire,
His wealth is not of earth to lose or get;
Earth reels, but he has stored his store above.

—*CHRISTINA ROSSETTI, 1830-1894*

AS OINTMENT POURED FORTH

Is this that Name as ointment poured forth
For which the virgins love Thee; King of kings
And Lord of lords? All seraphs clad in wings;
All Cherubs and all Wheels which south and north,
Which east and west turn not in going forth;
All many-semblanced ordered spirits, as rings
Of rainbow in unwonted fashionings,
Might answer, Yes. But we from south and north,
From east and west, a feeble folk who came
By desert ways in quest of land unseen,
A promised land of pasture ever green
And ever springing ever singing wave,
Know best Thy Name of Jesus: Blessed Name,
Man's life and resurrection from the grave.

—*CHRISTINA ROSSETTI, 1830-1894*

O! TELL ME, THOU LIFE AND DELIGHT OF MY SOUL!

O! tell me, Thou life and delight of my soul,
Where the flock of Thy pastures are feeding;
I seek Thy protection, I need Thy control,
I would go where my Shepherd is leading.

O! tell me the place where Thy flocks are at rest,
Where the noontide will find them reposing?
The tempest now rages, my soul is distress'd,
And the pathway of peace I am losing.

O! why should I stray with the flocks of Thy foes,
'Mid the desert where now they are roving,
Where hunger and thirst, where affliction and woes,
And temptations their ruin are proving!

O! when shall my foes and my wandering cease?
And the follies that fill me with weeping!
Thou Shepherd of Israel, restore me that peace
Thou dost give to the flock Thou art keeping.

A voice from the Shepherd now bids thee return
By the way where the footprints are lying:
No longer to wander, no longer to mourn;
O fair one, now homeward be flying!

—THOMAS HASTINGS, 1784-1872

THE FACE OF CHRIST

A rose, a lily, and the Face of Christ
Have all our hearts sufficed:
For He is Rose of Sharon nobly born,
Our Rose without a thorn;
And He is Lily of the Valley, He
Most sweet in purity.
But when we come to name Him as He is,
Godhead, Perfection, Bliss,
All tongues fall silent, while pure hearts alone
Complete their orison.

—CHRISTINA ROSSETTI, 1830-1894

CHRIST, WHOSE GLORY FILLS THE SKIES

Christ, whose glory fills the skies,
Christ, the true, the only light,
Sun of Righteousness, arise!
Triumph o'er the shades of night;
Day-spring from on high, be near!
Day-star, in my heart appear!

Dark and cheerless is the morn,
If Thy life is hid from me;
Joyless is the day's return,
Till Thy mercy's beams I see;
Till they inward light impart,
Warmth and gladness to my heart.

Visit, then, this soul of mine;
Pierce the gloom of sin and grief;
Fill me, radiant Sun divine;
Scatter all my unbelief;
More and more Thyself display,
Shining to the perfect day.

—CHARLES WESLEY, 1707-1788

JESU, HIGHEST HEAVEN'S COMPLETENESS

Jesu, highest heaven's completeness,
Name of music to the ear,
To the lips surpassing sweetness,
Wine the fainting heart to cheer.

Eating Thee, the soul may hunger,
Drinking, still athirst may be;
But for earthly food no longer,
Nor for any stream but Thee.

Jesu, all delight exceeding,
Only hope of heart distrest;
Weeping eyes and spirit mourning
Find in Thee a place of rest.

Stay, O Beauty uncreated,
Ever ancient, ever new;
Banish deeds of darkness hated,
With Thy sweetness all bedew.

Jesu, fairest blossom springing
From a maiden ever pure,
May our lips Thy praise be singing
While eternal years endure.

—*BERNARD OF CLAIRVAUX, 1091-1153*
Tr. Robert Campbell, 1814-1888

SHOW ME THY FACE

Show me Thy face—one transient gleam
Of loveliness divine,
And I shall never think or dream
Of other love save Thine:
All lesser light will darken quite,
All lower glories wane,
The beautiful of earth will scarce
Seem beautiful again.

Show me Thy face—my faith and love
Shall henceforth fixed be,
And nothing here have power to move
My soul's serenity.
My life shall seem a trance, a dream,
And all I feel and see,
Illusive, visionary—Thou
The one reality!

Show me Thy face—I shall forget
The weary days of yore,
The fretting ghosts of vain regret
Shall haunt my soul no more.
All doubts and fears for future years
In quiet trust subside,
And naught but blest content and calm
Within my breast abide.

Show me Thy face—the heaviest cross
Will then seem light to bear;
There will be gain in every loss,
And peace with every care.
With such light feet the years will fleet,
Life seem as brief as blest,
Till I have laid my burden down,
And entered into rest.

—AUTHOR UNKNOWN

NONE OTHER LAMB, NONE OTHER NAME

None other Lamb, none other Name,
None other Hope in heaven or earth or sea,
None other Hiding-place from guilt and shame,
None beside Thee.

My faith burns low, my hope burns low;
Only my heart's desire cries out in me,
By the deep thunder of its want and woe,
Cries out to Thee.

Lord, Thou art Life, though I be dead;
Love's Fire Thou art, however cold I be:
Nor heaven have I, nor place to lay my head,
Nor home, but Thee.

—*CHRLSTINA ROSSETTI, 1830-1894*

ASPIRATIONS OF THE SOUL AFTER CHRIST

My Spouse! in whose presence I live,
Sole object of all my desires,
Who know'st what a flame I conceive,
And canst easily double its fires;
How pleasant is all that I meet!
From fear of adversity free,
I find even sorrow made sweet,
Because 'tis assign'd me by Thee.

Transported I see Thee display
Thy riches and glory divine;
I have only my life to repay,
Take what I would gladly resign.
Thy will is the treasure I seek,
For Thou art as faithful as strong;
There let me, obedient and meek,
Repose myself all the day long.

My spirit and faculties fail;
Oh finish what Love has begun!
Destroy what is sinful and frail,
And dwell in the soul Thou hast won!
Dear theme of my wonder and praise,
I cry, who is worthy as Thou!
I can only be silent and gaze;
'Tis all that is left to me now.

Oh glory, in which I am lost,
Too deep for the plummet of thought!
On an ocean of Deity toss'd,
I am swallow'd, I sink into nought.

Yet lost and absorb'd as I seem,
I chant to the praise of my King;
And though overwhelm'd by the theme,
Am happy whenever I sing.

—JEANNE MARIE DE LA MOTTE-GUYON, 1648-1718
Tr. Unknown

THE PAIN OF LOVE

Jesus! why dost Thou love me so?
What hast Thou seen in me
To make my happiness so great,
So dear a joy to Thee?

Wert Thou not God, I then might think
Thou hadst no eye to read
The badness of that selfish heart,
For which Thine own did bleed.

But Thou art God, and knowest all;
Dear Lord! Thou knowest me;
And yet Thy knowledge hinders not
Thy love's sweet liberty.

Ah, how Thy grace hath wooed my soul
With persevering wiles!
Now give me tears to weep; for tears
Are deeper joy than smiles.

Each proof renewed of Thy great love
Humbles me more and more,
And brings to light forgotten sins,
And lays them at my door.

The more I love Thee, Lord! the more
I hate my own cold heart;
The more Thou woundest me with love;
The more I feel the smart.

What shall I do, then, dearest Lord!
Say, shall I fly from Thee,
And hide my poor unloving self
Where Thou canst never see?

Or shall I pray that Thy dear love
To me might not be given?
Ah, no! love must be pain on earth,
If it be bliss in heaven.

—FREDERICK WILLIAM FABER, 1814-1863

THOU HIDDEN SOURCE OF CALM REPOSE

Thou hidden Source of calm repose,
Thou all-sufficient Love Divine,
My help and refuge from my foes,
Secure I am, if Thou art mine;
And lo! from sin, and grief, and shame,
I hide me, Jesus, in Thy Name.

Thy mighty Name salvation is,
And keeps my happy soul above;
Comfort it brings, and power, and peace,
And joy, and everlasting love;
To me, with Thy dear Name, are given
Pardon, and holiness, and heaven.

Jesus, my all in all Thou art;
My rest in toil, my ease in pain,
The medicine of my broken heart;
In war my peace, in loss my gain,
My smile beneath the tyrant's frown,
In shame my glory and my crown:

In want my plentiful supply,
In weakness my almighty power;
In bonds my perfect liberty,
My light in Satan's darkest hour;
My joy in grief, my shield in strife,
In death my everlasting life.

—CHARLES WESLEY, 1707-1788

THE MAN DIVINE

In the Paradise of glory
Is the Man Divine;
There my heart, O God, is tasting
Fellowship with Thine.

Called to share Thy joy unmeasured,
Now is heaven begun;
I rejoice with Thee, O Father,
In Thy glorious Son.

Where the heart of God is resting,
I have found my rest;
Christ who found me in the desert,
Laid me on His breast.

There in deep unhindered fulness
Doth my joy flow free—
On through everlasting ages,
Lord, beholding Thee.

Round me is creation groaning,
Death, and sin, and care;
But there is a rest remaining,
And my Lord is there.

There I find a blessed stillness
In His courts of love;
All below but strife and darkness,
Cloudless peace above.

'Tis a solitary pathway
To that fair retreat—
Where in deep and sweet communion
Sit I at His feet.

In that glorious isolation,
Loneliness how blest,
From the windy storm and tempest
Have I found my rest.

Learning from Thy lips for ever
All the Father's heart,
Thou hast, in that joy eternal,
Chosen me my part.

There, where Jesus, Jesus only,
Fills each heart and tongue,
Where Himself is all the radiance
And Himself the song.

Here, who follows Him the nearest,
Needs must walk alone;
There like many seas the chorus,
Praise surrounds the throne.

Here a dark and silent pathway;
In those courts so fair
Countless hosts, yet each beholding
Jesus only, there.

—"T. P."

THEE WILL I LOVE

Thee will I love, my Strength, my Tower,
Thee will I love, my Joy, my Crown,
Thee will I love with all my power,
In all Thy works, and Thee alone;
Thee will I love, till the pure fire
Fill my whole soul with chaste desire.

Ah, why did I so late Thee know,
Thee, lovelier than the sons of men!
Ah, why did I no sooner go
To Thee, the only ease in pain!
Ashamed, I sigh, and inly mourn,
That I so late to Thee did turn.

I thank Thee, uncreated Sun,
That Thy bright beams on me have shined;
I thank Thee, who hast overthrown
My foes, and healed my wounded mind;
I thank Thee, whose enlivening voice
Bids my freed heart in Thee rejoice.

Uphold me in the doubtful race,
Nor suffer me again to stray;
Strengthen my feet with steady pace
Still to press forward in Thy way;
My soul and flesh, O Lord of might,
Fill, satiate, with Thy heavenly light.

Give to mine eyes refreshing tears,
Give to my heart chaste, hallowed fires,
Give to my soul, with filial fires,
The love that all heaven's host inspires;
That all my powers, with all their might,
In Thy sole glory may unite.

Thee will I love, my Joy, my Crown,
Thee will I love, my Lord, my God;
Thee will I love, beneath Thy frown,
Or smile, Thy sceptre, or Thy rod;
What though my flesh and heart decay,
Thee shall I love in endless day.

—JOHANN SCHEFFLER, 1624-1677
Tr. John Wesley, 1703-1791

AT THE LORD'S TABLE

Here, O my Lord, I see Thee face to face;
Here would I touch and handle things unseen,
Here grasp with firmer hand the eternal grace,
And all my weariness upon Thee lean.

Here would I feed upon the bread of God,
Here drink with Thee the royal wine of heaven;
Here would I lay aside each earthly load,
Here taste afresh the calm of sin forgiven.

This is the hour of banquet and of song;
This is the heavenly table spread for me;
Here let me feast, and feasting, still prolong
The brief bright hour of fellowship with Thee.

Too soon we rise; the symbols disappear;
The feast, though not the love, is past and gone;
The bread and wine remove, but Thou art here,
Nearer than ever; still my Shield and Sun.

I have no help but Thine; nor do I need
Another arm save Thine to lean upon;
It is enough, my Lord, enough indeed;
My strength is in Thy might, Thy might alone.

Mine is the sin, but Thine the righteousness;
Mine is the guilt, but Thine the cleansing blood;
Here is my robe, my refuge, and my peace, —
Thy blood, Thy righteousness, O Lord my God.

Feast after feast thus comes and passes by,
Yet, passing, points to the glad feast above,
Giving sweet foretaste of the festal joy,
The Lamb's great bridal feast of bliss and love.

—HORATIUS BONAR, 1808-1889

PRAYER BEFORE COMMUNION

Bread of the world, in mercy broken,
Wine of the soul, in mercy shed,
By whom the words of life were spoken,
And in whose death our sins are dead:
Look on the heart by sorrow broken,
Look on the tears by sinners shed;
And be Thy feast to us the token
That by Thy grace our souls are fed.

—REGINALD HEBER, 1783-1826

THE INDWELLING CHRIST

Thou who givest of Thy gladness
Till the cup runs o'er—
Cup whereof the pilgrim weary
Drinks to thirst no more—
Not a-nigh me, but within me
Is Thy joy divine;
Thou, O Lord, hast made Thy dwelling
In this heart of mine.

Need I that a law should bind me
Captive unto Thee?
Captive is my heart, rejoicing
Never to be free.
Ever with me, glorious, awful,
Tender, passing sweet,
One upon whose heart I rest me,
Worship at His Feet.

With me, wheresoe'er I wander,
That great Presence goes,
That unutterable gladness,
Undisturbed repose.
Everywhere the blessed stillness
Of His Holy Place—
Stillness of the love that worships
Dumb before His Face.

To Thy house, O God my Father,
Thy lost child is come;
Led by wandering lights no longer,
I have found my home.
Over moor and fen I tracked them
Through the midnight blast,
But to find the Light eternal
In my heart at last.

—GERHARD TERSTEEGEN, 1697-1769
Tr. Unknown

AS INCENSE STREAMING FORTH

Thy Name, O Christ, as incense streaming forth
Sweetens our names before God's Holy Face;
Luring us from the south and from the north
Unto the sacred place.

In Thee God's promise is Amen and Yea.
What art Thou to us? Prize of every lot,
Shepherd and Door, our Life and Truth and Way:—
Nay, Lord, what art Thou not?

—CHRISTINA ROSSETTI, 1830-1894

HOSANNA, LORD!

Hosanna to the living Lord!
Hosanna to th' incarnate Word!
To Christ, Creator, Saviour, King,
Let earth, let heaven, Hosanna sing!

Hosanna, Lord! Thine angels cry;
Hosanna, Lord! Thy saints reply;
Above, beneath us, and around,
The dead and living swell the sound.

O Saviour, with protecting care,
Return to this Thy house of prayer:
Where we Thy parting promise claim:
Assembled in Thy sacred Name.

But, chiefest, in our cleansed breast,
Eternal! bid Thy Spirit rest;
And make our secret soul to be
A temple pure, and worthy Thee.

So in the last and dreadful day,
When earth and heaven shall melt away,
Thy flock, redeemed from sinful stain,
Shall swell the sound of praise again.

—*REGINALD HEBER, 1783-1826*

AM I NOT ENOUGH?

Am I not enough, Mine own? enough,
Mine own, for thee?
Hath the world its palace towers,
Garden glades of magic flowers,
Where thou fain wouldst be?
Fair things and false are there,
False things but fair.
All shalt thou find at last,
Only in Me.
Am I not enough, Mine own? I, for ever
and alone, I, needing thee?

—GERHARD TERSTEEGEN, 1697-1769
Tr. Unknown

JESUS, THOU JOY OF LOVING HEARTS

Jesus, Thou Joy of loving hearts,
Thou Fount of life, Thou Light of men,
From the best bliss that earth imparts
We turn unfilled to Thee again.

Thy truth unchanged hath ever stood;
Thou savest those that on Thee call:
To them that seek Thee Thou art good,
To them that find Thee, all in all.

We taste Thee, O Thou living Bread,
And long to feast upon Thee still;
We drink of Thee, the Fountain-head,
And thirst our souls from Thee to fill.

Our restless spirits yearn for Thee,
Where'er our changeful lot is cast, —
Glad when Thy gracious smile we see,
Blest when our faith can hold Thee fast.

O Jesus, ever with us stay;
Make all our moments calm and bright;
Chase the dark night of sin away;
Shed o'er the world Thy holy light.

—BERNARD OF CLAIRVAUX, 1091-1153
Tr. Ray Palmer, 1808-1887

JOYOUS ANTICIPATION OF CHRIST'S RETURN

WAKE, AWAKE, FOR NIGHT IS FLYING

"Wake, awake, for night is flying,"
The watchmen on the heights are crying;
"Awake, Jerusalem, at last!"
Midnight hears the welcome voices,
And at the thrilling cry rejoices:
"Come forth, ye virgins, night is past!
The Bride-groom comes, awake,
Your lamps with gladness take;
Hallelujah!
And for His marriage feast prepare,
For ye must go to meet Him there."

Zion hears the watchmen singing,
And all her heart with joy is springing;
She wakes, she rises from her gloom;
For her Lord comes down all glorious,
The strong in grace, in truth victorious,
Her Star is risen, her Light is come!
Ah come, Thou blessed Lord,
O Jesus, Son of God,
Hallelujah!
We follow till the halls we see
Where Thou hast bid us sup with Thee.

Now let all the heavens adore Thee,
And men and angels sing before Thee,
With harp and cymbal's clearest tone;
Of one pearl each shining portal,
Where we are with the choir immortal
Of angels round Thy dazzling throne;
Nor eye bath seen, nor ear
Hath yet attained to hear,
What there is ours;
But we rejoice, and sing to Thee
Our hymns of joy eternally.

—*PHILIPP NICOLAI, 1556-1608*
Tr. Catherine Winkworth, 1829-1878

LO! HE COMES!

Lo! He comes, with clouds descending,
Once for favored sinners slain:
Thousand thousand saints attending,
Swell the triumph of His train:
Hallelujah!
God appears on earth to reign!

See the universe in motion,
Sinking on her funeral pyre—
Earth dissolving, and the ocean
Vanishing in final fire:
Hark the trumpet!
Loud proclaims the Day of Ire!

Graves have yawned in countless numbers,
From the dust the dead arise;
Millions out of silent slumbers,
Wake in overwhelmed surprise;
Where creation
Wrecked and torn on ruin lies!

See the Judge our nature wearing,
Pure, ineffable, divine:

See the great Archangel bearing
High in heaven the mystic sign:
Cross of Glory!
Christ be in that moment mine!

Every eye shall now behold Him
Robed in dreadful majesty;
Those who set aside and sold Him,
Pierced and nailed Him to the tree,
Deeply wailing,
Shall the true Messiah see.

All the tokens of His passion
Still His dazzling body bears;
Cause of endless exultation
To His ransomed worshippers;
With what rapture
Gaze we on those glorious scars.

Lo! the last long separation!
As the cleaving crowds divide;
And one dread adjudication
Sends each soul to either side!
Lord of mercy!
How shall I that day abide!

O, may Thine own Bride and Spirit
Then avert a dreadful doom,
And me summon to inherit
An eternal blissful home:—
Ah! come quickly!
Let Thy second advent come!

Yea, Amen! Let all adore Thee
High on Thine eternal throne!
Saviour—take the power and glory;
Make Thy righteous sentence known:
Jah! Jehovah!
Claim the kingdom for Thine own.

—JOHN CENNICK, et al. 1718-1755

THE HOPE OF HIS COMING

There is a balm for every pain,
A medicine for all sorrow;
The eye turned backward to the Cross,
And forward to the morrow.

The morrow of the glory and the psalm,
When He shall come;
The morrow of the harping and the palm,
The welcome home.
Meantime in His beloved hands our ways,
And on His Heart the wandering heart at rest;
And comfort for the weary one who lays
His head upon His Breast.

—GERHARD TERSTEEGEN, 1697-1769
Tr. Unknown

THE BLESSED MORROW

'Midst the darkness, storm, and sorrow,
One bright gleam I see;
Well I know the blessed morrow
Christ will come for me.
'Midst the light, and peace, and glory,
Of the Father's home,
Christ for me is watching, waiting,
Waiting till I come.

Long the blessed Guide has led me
By the desert road;
Now I see the golden towers,
City of my God.
There, amidst the love and glory,
He is waiting yet;
On His hands a name is graven
He can ne'er forget.

There, amidst the songs of heaven,
Sweeter to His ear
Is the footfall through the desert,
Ever drawing near.
There, made ready are the mansions,
Radiant, still, and fair;
But the Bride the Father gave Him
Yet is wanting there.

Who is this who comes to meet me
On the desert way,
As the Morning Star foretelling
God's unclouded day?
He it is who came to win me
On the Cross of shame;
In His glory well I know Him
Evermore the same.

Oh the blessed joy of meeting,
All the desert past!
Oh the wondrous words of greeting
He shall speak at last!
He and I together entering
Those fair courts above—
He and I together sharing
All the Father's love.

Where no shade nor stain can enter,
Nor the gold be dim,
In that holiness unsullied,
I shall walk with Him.
Meet companion then for Jesus,
From Him, for Him, made—
Glory of God's grace for ever
There in me displayed.

He who in His hour of sorrow
Bore the curse alone;
I who through the lonely desert
Trod where He had gone;
He and I, in that bright glory,
One deep joy shall share—
Mine, to be for ever with Him;
His, that I am there.

—*GERHARD TERSTEEGEN, 1697-1769*
Tr. Unknown

IMMORTALITY AND THE WORLD TO COME

LIFT YOUR GLAD VOICES

Lift your glad voices in triumph on high,
For Jesus hath risen, and man cannot die.
Vain were the terrors that gathered around Him,
And short the dominion of death and the grave;
He burst from the fetters of darkness that bound Him,
Resplendent in glory, to live and to save.
Loud was the chorus of angels on high, —
"The Saviour hath risen, and man shall not die."

Glory to God, in full anthems of joy;
The being He gave us, death cannot destroy.
Sad were the life we must part with tomorrow,
If tears were our birthright, and death were our end;
But Jesus hath cheered the dark valley of sorrow,
And bade us, immortal, to heaven ascend.
Lift, then, your voices in triumph on high,
For Jesus hath risen, and man shall not die.

—HENRY WARE, 1794-1843

JESUS LIVES, AND SO SHALL I

Jesus lives, and so shall I.
Death! thy sting is gone forever:
He, who deigned for me to die,

Lives, the bands of death to sever.
He shall raise me with the just:
Jesus is my Hope and Trust.

Jesus lives and reigns supreme;
And, His kingdom still remaining,
I shall also be with Him,
Ever living, ever reigning.
God has promised; be it must:
Jesus is my Hope and Trust.

Jesus lives, and God extends
Grace to each returning sinner;
Rebels He receives as friends,
And exalts to highest honor.
God is True as He is Just;
Jesus is my Hope and Trust.

Jesus lives, and by His grace,
Victory o'er my passions giving,
I will cleanse my heart and ways,
Ever to His glory living.
The weak He raises from the dust:
Jesus is my Hope and Trust.

Jesus lives, and I am sure
Naught shall e'er from Jesus sever,
Satan's wiles, and Satan's power,
Pain or pleasure—ye shall never!
Christian armor can not rust:
Jesus is my Hope and Trust.

Jesus lives, and death is now
But my entrance into glory.
Courage! then, my soul, for thou
Hast a crown of life before thee;
Thou shalt find thy hopes were just—
Jesus is the Christian's Trust.

—CHRISTIAN F. GELLERT, 1715-1769
Tr. Unknown

O SING HALLELUJAH!

Our Lord Christ hath risen!
The tempter is foiled;
His legions are scattered,
His strongholds are spoiled.
O sing Hallelujah! O sing Hallelujah!
O sing Hallelujah, be joyful and sing,
Our great foe is baffled—Christ Jesus is King!

O sin, thou art vanquished,
Thy long reign is o'er;
Though still thou dost vex us,
We dread thee no more.
O sing Hallelujah! O sing Hallelujah!
O sing Hallelujah, be joyful and sing,
Who now can condemn us? Christ Jesus is King!

O death we defy thee!
A stronger than thou
Hath entered thy palace;
We fear thee not now!
O sing Hallelujah! O sing Hallelujah!
O sing Hallelujah, be joyful and sing,
The grave cannot scare us—Christ Jesus is King!

Our Lord Christ hath risen!
Day breaketh at last;
The long night of weeping
Is now well-nigh past.
O sing Hallelujah! O sing Hallelujah!
O sing Hallelujah, be joyful and sing,
Our foes are all conquered—Christ Jesus is King!

—*LORD PLUNKET—BISHOP OF MEATH, 1629-1681*

THOSE ENDLESS SABBATHS

O what their joy and their glory must be,
Those endless Sabbaths the blessed ones see!
Crown for the valiant; to weary ones rest;
God shall be all, and in all ever blest.

What are the Monarch, His court, and His throne?
What are the peace and the joy that they own?
Tell us, ye blest ones, that in it have share,
If what ye feel ye can fully declare.

Truly Jerusalem name we that shore,
"Vision of peace," that brings joy evermore!
Wish and fulfilment can severed be ne'er,
Nor the thing prayed for come short of the prayer.

We, where no trouble distraction can bring,
Safely the anthems of Zion shall sing;
While for Thy grace, Lord, their voices of praise
Thy blessed people shall evermore raise.

Low before Him with our praises we fall,
Of whom, and in whom, and through whom are all;
Of whom, the Father; and through whom, the Son;
In whom, the Spirit, with these ever One.

—PIERRE ABELARD, 1079-1142
Tr. John Mason Neale, 1818-1866

IN IMMANUEL'S LAND

The sands of time are sinking,
The dawn of Heaven breaks,
The summer morn I've sighed for,
The fair sweet morn awakes:
Dark, dark hath been the midnight,
But dayspring is at hand,
And glory—glory dwelleth
In Immanuel's land.

Oh! well it is for ever,
Oh! well for evermore,
My nest hung in no forest
Of all this death-doom'd shore:
Yea, let the vain world vanish,
As from the ship the strand,
While glory—glory dwelleth
In Immanuel's land.

There the Red Rose of Sharon
Unfolds its heartsome bloom,
And fills the air of Heaven
With ravishing perfume:—
Oh! to behold it blossom,
While by its fragrance farm'd
Where glory—glory dwelleth
In Immanuel's land.

The King there in His beauty,
Without a veil, is seen:
It were a well-spent journey,
Though seven deaths lay between.
The Lamb, with His fair army,
Doth on Mount Zion stand,
And glory—glory dwelleth
In Immanuel's land.

Oh! Christ He is the Fountain,
The deep sweet well of love!
The streams on earth I've tasted,
More deep I'll drink above:
There, to an ocean fulness,
His mercy doth expand,
And glory—glory dwelleth
In Immanuel's land.

E'en Anwoth was not heaven—
E'en preaching was not Christ;
And in my sea-beat prison
My Lord and I held tryst:
And aye my murkiest storm-cloud
Was by a rainbow spann'd,

Caught from the glory dwelling
In Immanuel's land.

But that He built a heaven
Of His surpassing love,
A little New Jerusalem,
Like to the one above,—
"Lord, take me o'er the water,"
Had been my loud demand,
"Take me to love's own country,
Unto Immanuel's land."

But flowers need night's cool darkness
The moonlight and the dew;
So Christ, from one who loved it,
His shining oft withdrew;
And then for cause of absence,
My troubled soul I scann'd—
But glory, shadeless, shineth
In Immanuel's land.

The little birds of Anwoth
I used to count them blest,—
Now, beside happier altars
I go to build my nest:
O'er these there broods no silence,
No graves around them stand,
For glory, deathless, dwelleth
In Immanuel's land.

Fair Anwoth by the Solway,
To me thou still art dear!
E'en from the verge of Heaven
I drop for thee a tear.
Oh! if one soul from Anwoth
Meet me at God's right hand,
My Heaven will be two Heavens,
In Immanuel's land.

I have wrestled on toward Heaven,
'Gainst storm, and wind, and tide:—
Now, like a weary traveller,

That leaneth on his guide,
Amid the shades of evening,
While sinks life's ling'ring sand,
I hail the glory dawning
From Immanuel's land.

Deep water cross'd life's pathway,
The hedge of thorns was sharp;
Now these lie all behind me—
Oh! for a well-tuned harp!
Oh! to join Hallelujah
With yon triumphant band,
Who sing, where glory dwelleth,
In Immanuel's land.

With mercy and with judgment
My web of time He wove,
And aye the dews of sorrow
Were lustered with His love.
I'll bless the hand that guided,
I'll bless the heart that plann'd,
When throned where glory dwelleth
In Immanuel's land.

Soon shall the cup of glory
Wash down earth's bitterest woes,
Soon shall the desert-briar
Break into Eden's rose:
The curse shall change to blessing—
The name on earth that's bann'd,
Be graven on the white stone
In Immanuel's land.
Oh! I am my Beloved's,
And my Beloved is mine!
He brings a poor vile sinner
Into His "House of wine."
I stand upon His merit,
I know no other stand,
Not e'en where glory dwelleth
In Immanuel's land.

I shall sleep sound in Jesus,
Fill'd with His likeness rise,
To live and to adore Him,
To see Him with these eyes
'Tween me and resurrection
But Paradise doth stand;
Then—then for glory dwelling
In Immanuel's land!

The Bride eyes not her garment,
But her dear Bridegroom's face;
I will not gaze at glory,
But on my King of Grace—
Not at the crown He giveth,
But on His pierced hand:
The Lamb is all the glory
Of Immanuel's land.

I have borne scorn and hatred,
I have borne wrong and shame,
Earth's proud ones have reproach'd me,
For Christ's thrice blessed name:—
Where God His seal set fairest
They've stamp'd their foulest brand;
But judgment shines like noonday
In Immanuel's land.

They've summoned me before them,
But there I may not come,—
My Lord says, "Come up hither,"
My Lord says, "Welcome Home!"
My kingly King, at His white throne,
My presence cloth command,
Where glory—glory dwelleth
In Immanuel's land.

—ANNE R. COUSIN, 1824-1906

THE CELESTIAL COUNTRY

The world is very evil,
The times are waxing late;
Be sober and keep vigil,
The Judge is at the gate—
The Judge that comes in mercy,
The Judge that comes with might,
To terminate the evil,
To diadem the right.
When the just and gentle Monarch
Shall summon from the tomb,
Let man, the guilty, tremble,
For Man, the God, shall doom!

Arise, arise, good Christian,
Let right to wrong succeed;
Let penitential sorrow
To heavenly gladness lead—
To the light that hath no evening,
That knows nor moon nor sun,
The light so new and golden,
The light that is but one.

And when the Sole-Begotten
Shall render up once more
The kingdom to the Father,
Whose own it was before,
Then glory yet unheard of
Shall shed abroad its ray,
Resolving all enigmas,
An endless Sabbath-day.

Then, then from his oppressors
The Hebrew shall go free,
And celebrate in triumph
The year of jubilee;
And the sunlit Land that recks not
Of tempest nor of fight,
Shall fold within its bosom
Each happy Israelite—
The Home of fadeless splendor,

Of flowers that fear no thorn,
Where they shall dwell as children,
Who here as exiles mourn.

Midst power that knows no limit,
And wisdom free from bound,
The Beatific Vision
Shall glad the Saints around—
The peace of all the faithful,
The calm of all the blest,
Inviolate, unvaried,
Divinest, sweetest, best.
Yes, peace! for war is needless—
Yes, calm! for storm is past—
And goal from finished labor,
And anchorage at last.

That peace—but who may claim it?
The guileless in their way,
Who keep the ranks of battle,
Who mean the thing they say—
The peace that is for heaven,
And shall be for the earth;
The palace that re-echoes
With festal song and mirth;
The garden, breathing spices,
The paradise on high;
Grace beautified to glory,
Unceasing minstrelsy.

There nothing can be feeble,
There none can ever mourn,
There nothing is divided,
There nothing can be torn.
'Tis fury, ill, and scandal,
'Tis peaceless peace below;
Peace, endless, strifeless, ageless,
The halls of Syon know.

O happy, holy portion,
Refection for the blest,
True vision of true beauty,

Sweet cure of all distrest!
Strive, man, to win that glory;
Toil, man, to gain that light;
Send hope before to grasp it,
Till hope be lost in sight;
Till Jesus gives the portion
Those blessed souls to fill—
The insatiate, yet satisfied,
The full, yet craving still.

That fulness and that craving
Alike are free from pain,
Where thou, midst heavenly citizens,
A home like theirs shalt gain.
Here is the warlike trumpet;
There, life set free from sin,
When to the last Great Supper
The faithful shall come in;
When the heavenly net is laden
With fishes many and great
(So glorious in its fulness,
Yet so inviolate);
And perfect from unperfected,
And fall'n from those that stand,
And the sheep-flock from the goat-herd
Shall part on either hand.

And these shall pass to torment,
And those shall triumph then—
The new peculiar nation,
Blest number of blest men.
Jerusalem demands them;
They paid the price on earth,
And now shall reap the harvest
In blissfulness and mirth—
The glorious holy people,
Who evermore relied
Upon their Chief and Father,
The King, the Crucified—
The sacred ransomed number
Now bright with endless sheen,
Who made the Cross their watchword

Of Jesus Nazarene,
Who (fed with heavenly nectar
Where soul-like odors play)
Draw out the endless leisure
Of that long vernal day.

And, through the sacred lilies
And flowers on every side,
The happy dear-bought people
Go wandering far and wide;
Their breasts are filled with gladness,
Their mouths are tun'd to praise,
What time, now safe for ever,
On former sins they gaze:
The fouler was the error,
The sadder was the fall,
The ampler are the praises
Of Him who pardoned all.

Their one and only anthem,
The fulness of His love,
Who gives instead of torment,
Eternal joys above—
Instead of torment, glory;
Instead of death, that life
Wherewith your happy Country,
True Israelites, is rife.
Brief life is here our portion,
Brief sorrow, short-liv'd care;
The life that knows no ending—
The tearless life, is there.

O happy retribution!
Short toil, eternal rest;
For mortals and for sinners
A mansion with the blest!
That we should look, poor wand'rers,
To have our home on high!
That worms should seek for dwelling,
Beyond the starry sky!
To all one happy guerdon
Of one celestial grace;

For all, for all, who mourn their fall,
Is one eternal place.

And martyrdom hath roses
Upon that heavenly ground;
And white and virgin lilies
For virgin-souls abound.
There grief is turned to pleasure—
Such pleasure as below
No human voice can utter,
No human heart can know;
And after fleshly scandal,
And after this world's night,
And after storm and whirlwind,
Is calm, and joy, and light.

And now we fight the battle,
But then shall wear the crown
Of full and everlasting
And passionless renown:
And now we watch and struggle,
And now we live in hope,
And Syon, in her anguish,
With Babylon must cope;
But He whom now we trust in
Shall then be seen and known,
And they that know and see Him
Shall have Him for their own.

The miserable pleasures
Of the body shall decay;
The bland and flattering struggles
Of the flesh shall pass away;
And none shall there be jealous,
And none shall there contend;
Fraud, clamor, guile—what say I?
All ill, all ill shall end!
And there is David's Fountain,
And life in fullest glow;
And there the light is golden,
And milk and honey flow—
The light that hath no evening,

The health that hath no sore,
The life that hath no ending,
But lasteth evermore.

There Jesus shall embrace us,
There Jesus be embraced—
That spirit's food and sunshine
Whence earthly love is chased.
Amidst the happy chorus,
A place, however low,
Shall shew Him us, and shewing,
Shall satiate evermo.

By hope we struggle onward:
While here we must be fed
By milk, as tender infants,
But there by Living Bread.
The night was full of terror,
The morn is bright with gladness;
The Cross becomes our harbor,
And we triumph after sadness.

And Jesus to His true ones
Brings trophies fair to see;
And Jesus shall be loved, and
Beheld in Galilee—
Beheld, when morn shall waken,
And shadows shall decay,
And each true-hearted servant
Shall shine as doth the day;
And every ear shall hear it—
"Behold thy King's array,
Behold thy God in beauty,
The Law hath pass'd away!"
Yes! God my King and Portion,
In fulness of Thy grace,
We then shall see for ever,
And worship face to face.
Then Jacob into Israel,
From earthlier self estranged,
And Leah into Rachel
For ever shall be changed;

Then all the halls of Syon
For aye shall be complete,
And in the Land of Beauty,
All things of beauty meet.

For thee, O dear, dear Country!
Mine eyes their vigils keep;
For very love, beholding
Thy happy name, they weep.
The mention of thy glory
Is unction to the breast,
And medicine in sickness,
and love, and life, and rest.
O One, O only Mansion!
O Paradise of Joy!
Where tears are ever banished,
And smiles have no alloy,
Beside thy living waters
All plants are, great and small,
The cedar of the forest,
The hyssop of the wall;
With jaspers glow thy bulwarks,
Thy streets with emeralds blaze,
The sardius and the topaz
Unite in thee their rays;
Thine ageless walls are bonded
With amethyst unpriced;
Thy Saints build up its fabric,
And the corner-stone is Christ.

The Cross is all thy splendor,
The Crucified thy praise;
His laud and benediction
Thy ransomed people raise:
"Jesus, the Gem of Beauty,
True God and Man," they sing,
"The never-failing Garden,
The ever-golden Ring;
The Door, the Pledge, the Husband,
The Guardian of his Court;
The Day-star of Salvation,
The Porter and the Port!"

Thou hast no shore, fair ocean!
Thou hast no time, bright day!
Dear fountain of refreshment
To pilgrims far away!
Upon the Rock of Ages
They raise thy holy tower;
Thine is the victor's laurel,
And thine the golden dower!
Thou feel'st in mystic rapture,
O Bride that know'st no guile,
The Prince's sweetest kisses,
The Prince's loveliest smile;
Unfading lilies, bracelets
Of living pearl thine own;
The Lamb is ever near thee,
The Bridegroom thine alone.
The Crown is He to guerdon,
The Buckler to protect,
And he Himself the Mansion,
And He the Architect.

The only art thou needest—
Thanksgiving for thy lot;
The only joy thou seekest—
The Life where Death is not.
And all thine endless leisure,
In sweetest accents, sings
The ill that was thy merit,
The wealth that is thy King's!

Jerusalem the golden,
With milk and honey blest,
Beneath thy contemplation
Sink heart and voice oppressed.
I know not, O I know not,
What social joys are there!
What radiancy of glory,
What light beyond compare!

And when I fain would sing them,
My spirit fails and faints;
And vainly would it image

The assembly of the Saints.
They stand, those halls of Syon,
Conjubilant with song,
And bright with many an angel,
And all the martyr throng;
The Prince is ever in them,
The daylight is serene;
The pastures of the Blessed
Are decked in glorious sheen.

There is the Throne of David,
And there, from care released,
The song of them that triumph,
The shout of them that feast;
And they who, with their Leader,
Have conquered in the fight,
For ever and for ever
Are clad in robes of white!

O holy, placid harp-notes
Of that eternal hymn!
O sacred, sweet refection,
And peace of Seraphim!
O thirst, for ever ardent,
Yet evermore content!
O true peculiar vision
Of God cunctipotent!
Ye know the many mansions
For many a glorious name,
And divers retributions
That divers merits claim;
For midst the constellations
That deck our earthly sky,
This star than that is brighter—
And so it is on high.
Jerusalem the glorious!
The glory of the Elect!
O dear and future vision
That eager hearts expect!
Even now by faith I see thee,
Even here thy walls discern;
To thee my thoughts are kindled,

And strive, and pant, and yearn.

Jerusalem the only,
That look'st from heaven below,
In thee is all my glory,
In me is all my woe;
And though my body may not,
My spirit seeks thee fain,
Till flesh and earth return me
To earth and flesh again.

O none can tell thy bulwarks,
How gloriously they rise!
O none can tell thy capitals
O beautiful device!
Thy loveliness oppresses
All human thought and heart;
And none, O peace, O Syon,
Can sing thee as thou art!

New mansion of new people,
Whom God's own love and light
Promote, increase, make holy,
Identify, unite!
Thou City of the Angels!
Thou City of the Lord!
Whose everlasting music
Is the glorious decachord!

And there the band of Prophets
United praise ascribes,
And there the twelvefold chorus
Of Israel's ransomed tribes,
The lily-beds of virgins,
The roses' martyr-glow,
The cohort of the Fathers
Who kept the Faith below.

And there the Sole-Begotten
Is Lord in regal state—
He, Judah's mystic Lion,
He, Lamb Immaculate.

O fields that know no sorrow!
O state that fears no strife!
O princely bowers! O land of flowers!
O realm and home of Life!

Jerusalem, exulting
On that securest shore,
I hope thee, wish thee, sing thee,
And love thee evermore!
I ask not for my merit,
I seek not to deny
My merit is destruction,
A child of wrath am I;
But yet with Faith I venture
And Hope upon my way;
For those perennial guerdons
I labor night and day.

The best and dearest Father,
Who made me and who saved,
Bore with me in defilement,
And from defilement laved,
When in His strength I struggle,
For very joy I leap,

When in my sin I totter,
I weep, or try to weep:
But grace, sweet grace celestial,
Shall all its love display,
And David's Royal Fountain
Purge every sin away.

O mine, my golden Syon!
O lovelier far than gold,
With laurel-girt battalions,
And safe victorious fold!
O sweet and blessed Country,
Shall I ever see thy face?
O sweet and blessed Country,
Shall I ever win thy grace?
I have the hope within me
To comfort and to bless!

Shall I ever win the prize itself?
O tell me, tell me, Yes!

Exult, O dust and ashes!
The Lord shall be thy part;
His only, His for ever,
Thou shalt be, and thou art!
Exult, O dust and ashes!
The Lord shall be thy part;
His only, His for ever,
Thou shalt be, and thou art!

—*BERNARD OF CLUNY, 12th Century*

NOTES

1. This hymn dates from the fourth century and is generally acknowledged to be one of the greatest ever written.

    As a night bird sings out of the darkness and we hear its song without locating its exact source, so the Te Deum sings out of the obscurity of the past. The author is not certainly known. Some have attributed the hymn to Ambrose, Bishop of Milan, but the weight of scholarly opinion would favor Nicetas, Bishop of Remesiana in Dacia.

    Whoever composed it, one thing is certain: it has through the centuries been for countless thousands of Christians a ringing affirmation of faith in God and an expression of complete confidence in Jesus Christ His Son. Here are found also confession of sin, ecstatic praise and a tender plea for mercy. Altogether it is theology aflame with devotion, and this we believe is an offering well pleasing to God.

2. This much-loved poem was composed by Mrs. Anne Ross Cousin, wife of a minister of the Free Church of Scotland. The poem is as remarkable as it is beautiful in that Mrs. Cousin extracted from the letters of Samuel Rutherford many of his most memorable sayings and wove them into a hymn of nineteen stanzas, maintaining throughout high poetic excellence and great faithfulness to the language and spirit of the letters.

    Certain stanzas of this poem are familiar to most Christians as "The Sands of Time Are Sinking."

3. Bernard of Cluny was born, probably of English parents, either at Morlaix (Brittany), or at Morlas, in the Pyrenees. Neither the exact time and place of his birth nor the date of his death is known with certainty.

    Bernard joined the Benedictine order and entered the Abbey of Cluny, in northern France. There about A. D. 1145 he wrote De Contemptu Mundi, a bold and merciless attack upon the moral and spiritual corruption of the world as found in society generally and in the Roman Church in particular. The outraged prophet spared nothing and no one, from the Pope down, but in words of burning eloquence set forth count after count in a terrible indictment of the Church as well as of the world. The whole long poem consists of about 3,000 lines.

About a hundred years ago Dr. John Mason Neale, the celebrated English scholar and linguist, turned a part of Bernard's poem into English verse. This work appears here under the title "The Celestial Country." It is my opinion that nothing in the English language remotely compares with this in its beautiful sorrow for earth and its rapturous description of heaven.

Here time and eternity are blended as the grief-stricken but enraptured monk shows us the ugliness of earth and the loveliness of heaven. As time fades away, eternity rises to gather all redeemed and blood-washed souls in an everlasting embrace of pure and perfect love. Here we find the triumphant answer to all questions concerning the chief end of man. Bernard knew the answer, and so do all who read sympathetically his lovely and inspired poem.

www.ingramcontent.com/pod-product-compliance
Lightning Source LLC
Chambersburg PA
CBHW021440070526
44577CB00002B/227